Samuel J. (Samuel June) Barrows

A Baptist Meeting-House

The Staircase to the old Faith; The open Door to the new

Samuel J. (Samuel June) Barrows

A Baptist Meeting-House
The Staircase to the old Faith; The open Door to the new

ISBN/EAN: 9783337152536

Printed in Europe, USA, Canada, Australia, Japan

Cover: Foto ©ninafisch / pixelio.de

More available books at **www.hansebooks.com**

A BAPTIST MEETING-HOUSE:

THE STAIRCASE TO THE OLD FAITH;
THE OPEN DOOR TO THE NEW.

BY

SAMUEL J. BARROWS.

"I have set before thee an open door, and no man can shut it."
Rev. iii. 8.

SECOND EDITION.

BOSTON:
AMERICAN UNITARIAN ASSOCIATION.
1890.

To the Memory

OF

A FAITHFUL AND BELOVED MOTHER.

PREFACE.

SOME eighteen months ago, while visiting New York, the writer caught a passing glimpse of the old church building which, when a young child, he attended with his mother. The fragrant recollections it awakened were embodied in an article in the "Christian Register." This article suggested a second, the second a third, until finally the series was continued to its natural conclusion. This involved not only a transcript of recollections, but a statement of experience. By the kind invitation of the American Unitarian Association, these articles have been revised and gathered together in the present volume, which, like the experience it describes, is an unpremeditated growth. The *nom de plume* which was used extemporaneously in the first article, it was found necessary to continue through the series. It has become so identified, therefore, with the growth of the book, that it seems best to retain it.

The writer is fully aware that there are important religious and philosophical problems confronting both Orthodoxy and Unitarianism which are not treated in this book. He has simply aimed to present those which he encountered in his transition from the old faith to the new. He has often been asked by friends of the communion which he left, what it was that led to such a complete change in his religious views, as if by some magical or miraculous process an instantaneous conversion had been effected. To such inquiries, the book itself is the best answer. Many who cannot accept its final conclusions may yet be induced to see the natural and successive steps by which religious convictions are developed.

It is seldom that two persons passing from one form of faith to another traverse precisely the same pathway; but the actual experience of one who has made the journey may not be without help to those who are on the road.

Grateful for all the nurture he received in the old household of faith, and equally grateful for the shelter and development he has received in the new, the writer humbly lays this tribute, the fruit of his experience, upon the altar of his religious faith.

S. J. B.

Boston, Mass., Sept. 17, 1885.

CONTENTS.

		PAGE
I.	AN UPPER ROOM	9
II.	THE INFANT CLASS	15
III.	THE SERMON GAUGE	25
IV.	THE TYPICAL MINISTER	34
V.	REVIVAL FIRES	42
VI.	FINDING PEACE	49
VII.	THE BAPTISM	55
VIII.	A BUSY CONVERT	64
IX.	THE PRAYER-MEETING	73
X.	GETTING THEOLOGY	83
XI.	AN INSIDE VIEW OF CALVINISM	92
XII.	TRANSITIONS	99
XIII.	A MILD CASE OF HERESY	108
XIV.	UNION AND COMMUNION	114
XV.	SUNDAY OBSERVANCE	122
XVI.	AN EFFECTIVE SERMON	127
XVII.	THREE LUMINOUS BOOKS	135
XVIII.	SEARCHING THE BIBLE, AND WHAT CAME OF IT	141

CONTENTS.

		PAGE
XIX.	WHAT THINK YE OF CHRIST?	150
XX.	A SIGNIFICANT LETTER.	159
XXI.	LABORING WITH A HERETIC	165
XXII.	EXCOMMUNICATED.	179
XXIII.	SEEKING A HOME	185
XXIV.	THE NEW HOME AND THE NEW FAITH	192
XXV.	CONCLUSION	211

BAPTIST MEETING-HOUSE.

I.

AN UPPER ROOM.

SCHLIEMANN, in his early excavations at the site of Troy, declared that there were several successive cities built on the top of each other and covered with the débris of the ages, an opinion which he afterward modified. Whether it be true or not of Troy, it is true at least that there have been several New Yorks, and that the New York of to-day, with its Broadway and elevated railroads, its East River Bridge, its electric lights, its Central Park, its palatial residences, its magnificent temples of worship and halls of trade, its boulevards, its enormous hotels and apartment houses, and its territorial growth from Harlem River to Yonkers, — the New York of to-day is but little like the New York of thirty years ago. Beyond this point the recollections of the writer do not reach very extensively; a trip to High Bridge, made six years before, being the earliest event which the memory has distinctly photographed. The oldest inhabitant, leaping as he may without crutches over an historic interval of seventy-five or eighty years, may smile at the juvenility of this reminiscence. He has mapped on his mind a still older New York, compared with which that city, as it existed in 1850, seems comparatively modern. Nevertheless, the New York of thirty years ago has been as completely overlaid by later growth as the city that preceded it.

In those days the era of millionnaires had not been ushered in. Two hundred thousand dollars, — yes, half that sum made a man rich! The aristocracy of birth ruled more than the aristocracy of wealth. The old Knickerbockers had not surrendered their hold upon social supremacy. New York, though rapidly yielding to other influences, still recognized its Dutch heritage. Wealth was not divorced from simplicity. Plain brick fronts on Greenwich Street, Bleecker Street, and East Broadway were good enough for the best. On the east side there were still reminders of the old colonial estates, such as Willets Garden in Delancey Street, and Rutgers Garden in Madison Street, in which old-fashioned mansions stood in the centre of the block, and were surrounded by gardens and groves covering nearly its whole extent. Rich and poor lived very close together. Capitalists did not disdain to live near their workingmen. The Battery and Castle Garden, and the Elysian Fields at Hoboken, were pleasure-resorts. Central Park was an uncultivated, rocky waste, inhabited by squatters and goats. On the east side market-gardens were found as low down as Fifth and Sixth Streets. Horse-cars had not covered the whole city with a grating of rails; the innovation was confined to a few streets. The Volunteer Fire Department was in all its glory. William M. Tweed — or "Bill Tweed," as he was familiarly known — blew the trumpet for "Six Engine;" and the boys of the neighborhood drew "the jumper," as the little hose-cart was called.

Ecclesiastically, New York presented, in its external features, a great contrast to the city of to-day. The up-town rush was threatening, but had not set in. Dr. Armitage preached in Norfolk Street, Dr. Hatfield in Broome Street. The Brick Church, near the old post-office, with Dr. Gardiner Spring as its pastor, and the Broadway Tabernacle, were centres of great interest. The most important churches in all denominations were down town.

But it is not around the most "important" churches, in any external sense, that the writer's recollections cluster. He is more concerned in recalling that which was important to him than what was important and influential in the city of New York. Three epochs are strongly indented in his memory; three churches loom up in connection with them. One of them reveals a picture of the first time he ever went to church; the second, a picture of the church and the Sunday-school which he attended in the most impressive years of childhood; the third is a fragrant memory of the church where, when yet a boy, his religious nature was first powerfully awakened. Two of these church organizations have long since been obliterated. Only one of the original buildings is still used as a church, and that is occupied by Germans.

The passenger on the Sixth Avenue elevated road may find the region between Prince and Houston Streets very uninteresting. Laurens Street, even when widened and dignified into South Fifth Avenue, is a region to be passed through as quickly as possible and without regret. Yet I seldom dash up town on the "Elevated" without trying to get a seat on the right-hand side of the car; and as we swiftly shoot from Grand to Bleecker Street, I catch a glimpse of two old wooden houses, joined by a little bridge at the top story. They have lapsed into a settled infirmity, and cannot long abide the ravages of time. In one of these twin houses — the connecting ligament suggesting the Siamese twins — was a large plain room, used as a place of worship by the Laurens Street Baptist Church. There was an apostolic simplicity in this upper room; and the organization and management of the church, of which I know but little, were based as nearly as possible upon apostolic models. Poverty was undoubtedly one of its attributes. The services were conducted from week to week by a beloved physician, Dr. Barker, who ministered to the souls of his people on Sundays, and to their bodies during the week. He would never take a penny for his preaching, and distributed his medicine to the poor with an equal generosity. He was tenderly loved by his people, and made an impression of gentleness and goodness upon a four-year-old boy that has never been erased.

One of the peculiarities of this church was the observance of the communion service every Sunday. It was a remarkable event in the life of a little boy, who received a

Hebrew name at his birth signifying "Asked-of-God,"[1] when his mother took him by the hand and led him across the city, a mile and three quarters, to this Baptist house of meeting. Only the most cloudy memories of the event remain. One incident comes out very definitely and clearly. When the bread and wine were passed to the communicants, the little boy cried bitterly because his mother would not let him partake. It may have been a phase of early piety; or was it early materialism?

How Asked-of-God's mother came to join the Baptist denomination I do not know, save that it was the result of profound conviction. Brought up in an old New York family of Dutch ancestry, sufficient means, and good position, it was a great shock to the members of her family, all of whom were socially or practically identified with the Dutch Reformed or Presbyterian churches, when she announced her intention of joining the Baptists. It might have seemed a trying step for a young girl to take, who had led the dance at the Firemen's Ball, a social event of that day, and whose overflowing gayety made her greatly sought in society. In the strength of her religious convictions, she probably never counted this a sacrifice; but it cut her to the heart when friends and kindred avoided her presence, and refused to speak to her. The ice was cut in the river for her baptism, but not one of her household witnessed the ceremony. Considering the method and the temperature, they may not have been wholly to blame

---

[1] Another and more literal rendering of the name is "Heard-of-God." But see 1 Sam. i. 20.

for declining to be present at a service in which the laws of health were somewhat violently affronted. A reconciliation afterward took place; but no other member of the family ever joined the Baptist fold, and it was a lifelong trial to a tender, loving spirit that by the laws of her church, to which she maintained a steadfast loyalty, she could not partake of the Lord's Supper with mother, brother, or sister.

When, in later years, Asked-of-God himself changed his theological relations, he recalled the fact that his mother had done so before him.

Only once does he remember attending that church. The distance was too great for little feet; and on the death of Dr. Barker, the enterprise was soon abandoned. But as he flits by on the railroad and takes an instantaneous view of that decrepit old house, it seems to be sanctified by the sweet aroma of a mother's prayers.

II.

THE INFANT CLASS.

THE church in which it was held was an unpretentious structure, without a bell and with two modest-looking turrets in place of a steeple. It could not vie in external appearance with St. Mary's, All Saints', or Rutgers Street Church. But one of those churches was Roman Catholic; another was Episcopalian, where the minister committed the grave offence of reading his prayers and preaching in a gown; and the third, if free from these unapostolic vices, was known to be devoid of a baptistery, while it observed the unscriptural practice of infant baptism. A little wooden Baptist Church with a pond under the pulpit was worth, in the eyes of this boy of seven, far more than any elaborate pile of brick and stone with a cross on it. The cross, in those youthful days, savored more of paganism than of Christianity.

This little church, like many others, was born of a feud. The history of the feud I have never traced; but I know it was a bitter one, — so bitter, indeed, that the parent church refused to allow the schismatic members to commune with them. The young church did not retaliate in this inhospitable fashion, but expressed its conciliatory spirit by taking as its name "The Olive Branch."

When Asked-of-God's mother withdrew from the Laurens Street Church, concerning which he has but the dimmest recollection, she cast her lot with this young and struggling society. It was not destined to have a long life, but for the writer it was a significant one. He began at the foot of the ladder, and entered the infant class in the Sunday-school. That infant class forms one of the brightest pictures in the memories of his youth. If there was anything irksome about it at the time, it is forgotten, together with most of the instruction which it weekly imparted. Baptist schools have never been much burdened with catechisms. The only thing in the shape of a catechism with which we were afflicted was a series of biographical epigrams concerning the most prominent characters of the Old Testament. It was asserted without fear of contradiction that Adam was the first man, the doctrine of evolution not yet having made its way into the Sunday-school. The only suspicion we had of the advent of any such hypothesis was when the Italian organ-grinder came around with his automaton figures and an accomplished monkey dressed in picturesque garments. The remarkable facial resemblance of the monkey to a boy in the school, whose agility and imitativeness helped also to win for him the distinction of this title, awakened childish suspicions that the relationship, though remote, was not without reality. The only other important moral and historical facts which I recall in this biographical catechism are that Cain was the first murderer; that Moses was the meekest man, and Methuselah the oldest; that Obadiah hid a hundred prophets in

THE INFANT CLASS. 17

a cave, and fed them on a meagre diet of bread and water; that Korah was swallowed by an earthquake, and that Elijah went up in a chariot of fire. So strongly were these facts impressed upon my memory that no prejudices of later education have been wholly able to remove them. Sceptics may argue that it is utterly impossible that Elijah should have done anything of the kind, and scientific men may interpose objections that are perfectly commanding to the reason. But still, for all this, the infant-school Elijah *did* ascend to heaven in a chariot of fire; and, in the mind of the writer, he still *continues* to ascend. And I hope he will never go to heaven in any other way. Imagine Elijah dying a natural death ! Nothing could be more prosaic.

The reason why this infant-school Elijah is perfectly safe against all the assaults of science, exegesis, and philosophy is that while these appeal to the rational nature, they cannot capture the imagination. It throws open its windows, and defies them. The best proof — in fact, the only proof — I have that Elijah so ascended to heaven is that I *can see him going.* Could anything be more conclusive? I have not the same certainty of conviction that he ever *reached* heaven. All that I know is that when I open my "windows toward Jerusalem," the old prophet, wrapped in a cloud of poetic glory, is still in the air. His fiery course is onward and upward; and though imagination refuses to portray his arrival in heaven, the picture of his ascension is always accompanied by the assurance that he will eventually get there.

I am thankful, as I look back into the rosy dawn of

these early memories, that we were never subjected to the didactic dreariness of the Shorter Catechism, or any other catechism, for that matter, but the brief biographical one of which I have spoken. The memory of no hard, dry dogma is connected with those days. Moral truths were not presented in axioms or precepts, but rather through historical and mythical examples. Our teacher would have been shocked enough, if told that any of the incidents in the lives of Hebrew saints were imaginary; but the fact remains that, whether conscious of it or not, she constantly appealed to the imagination in conveying moral truth. It requires an effort of the imagination to realize Joseph and Moses as certainly as to realize Samson or Jonah. As I look back, I cannot discover that there was any difference in the degree of reality with which they seemed invested. The question of credibility did not arise. The critical faculty was not awakened, and any and all of the Hebrew giants would have been admitted to confidence on the simple word of our teacher that they were worthy of it. If told that Adam was made so tall that his head touched the sky, as the rabbis say, or that the tower of Babel was fifty-six miles high, or that Abraham sucked milk from the forefinger of Gabriel, as the same authorities relate, the statement would not have seemed any more remarkable than other Hebrew legends, which say that the first woman was made from a rib of the first man, that a certain Hebrew grandfather lived to be nine hundred and thirty-six years old, or that the confusion of tongues began at Babel.

The imagination of the child was exceedingly hospitable. The consequence was that it readily accepted imaginative creations. Even Jonah was not excluded from the society of fellow-marvels. Though floating in an entirely different element from that of Elijah, his experience seemed quite as real. The fact that whales have small throats was not known in that infant class. It would have made no difference if it had been. The imagination would have created a fish large enough, and a Jonah small enough to vindicate the possibility. And this it repeatedly did. Let no modern heretic smile that the case of Jonah awakened at once the most active sympathies of the childish heart. That he deserved to be cast overboard and swallowed by a monster fish was not to be doubted, for the judgments of God were assumed to be altogether just. But the condition of the swallowed prophet was one that excited profound pity. I can see him to-day sitting with his back against the whale's ribs, a picture of loneliness and dejection, yet bearing with uncomplaining fortitude the miseries of his lot. Asked-of-God never saw Jonah in this sad condition without wishing to help him out. The imagination exerted its puny skill in vain efforts for his prompt release, but was generally obliged to fall back on the Scriptural device of a whalish fit of sickness. A few years later, when Baron Munchausen was eagerly read, the miraculous features of Jonah's history shrank into modest proportions compared with the extraordinary experience of the baron when entombed in a fish large enough to swallow a whole ship.

The value of this infant-class teaching, with its old-time miracles and marvels, its visions, exploits, deliverances, and catastrophes, its hoary-headed prophets and heroes, lay in a totally different direction perhaps from that in which it was estimated by our teachers. It opened to the child-mind a section of the great world of Hebrew tradition. It invested the past with a poetic glow; it awakened the sentiment of the sublime and the mysterious. As I look back, I should be very sorry if this mythological element had been left out of that infant-class instruction. My criticism would rather be that there was not more of it, that it was too narrow and special. The Old Testament stories might have been supplemented by other Semitic traditions from the Talmud relating to the same characters and events, and furnishing many interesting and even more extraordinary particulars. But such comparative and additional material was not so accessible then as it is now, and the whole world of Grecian myth was religiously supposed to be a world of falsehood. The advantage of a wider selection of stories, many of them embodying the same truths, would have been that the child would unconsciously have obtained a broader and better conception of the character of a myth, and been able, sooner or later, to separate fact from myth without doing violence to the religious sentiment. As it was, a great struggle ensued at a later period, when the critical faculty summoned these mythical characters and events to its judgment-seat, and would have remanded them all to the limbo of effete superstitions, had not the imagination wrapped them in its protecting fancies, and borne them aloft to its pantheon.

But the strongest and sweetest impression which I bring away from that infant class was not that made by a remote and mythical world. The Hebrew characters, to the child mind, were heroes; but they were not saints. The Hebrew God was a jealous, masculine embodiment of gigantic power and stern self-righteousness. The tender Jesus and the loving John, though familiar names, were not precious inspirations until the infant class was outgrown. But the ideal of goodness, sweetness, purity, and tenderness did not remain dormant. There was no need to look to the ancient world for its illustration. It was beautifully and winningly embodied in the life and character of a beloved teacher. It was she who made goodness real and virtue lovely. Her character was one which was not only good enough for heaven, but, tried by a higher and more exacting standard, was good enough for this world. There was no danger that the child-mind would ever lose its hold on the present life by a too fond admiration of that which was past. By an unconscious and irresistible attraction, she drew us back again from the old dream-world into the living present through the charm of her saintly womanhood. Here was a beautiful blending of veneration, spirituality, and affection in an actual, tangible human being, in a woman who spoke and sung and smiled. Other characters might be mythic, but this was indisputably real. The Hebrew worthies whom we were taught to revere were all masculine. There was not, then, a womanly figure among them to command our love or admiration. But the child mind and heart had other resources. It needed not to spell out, letter by letter, the old Hebrew Word; it could recognize the Word made flesh and dwelling among us. Here was a living exposition of that doctrine of the incarnation, whose genesis we can never find and whose revelation we can never limit. Here was a human embodiment of those feminine qualities of tenderness and love which were so lacking in the old Hebrew heroes and in the Hebrew God. The child had not then grasped the great truth of God manifest in the flesh, — that truth which not only appears in Jesus, but in all the other saviors of the world. God at that time dwelt in the sky. He was intensely personal. All considerations of time and space would have forbidden the belief that he dwelt anywhere but on his throne in heaven. It never occurred to the boy to think of him as dwelling in that purified human temple. He only knew that this alluring superexcellence was the superexcellence of goodness, and that it was the goodness of kind, tender, patient, lovable Mrs. Bruce.

But though God did not literally dwell with Mrs. Bruce, the boy had a firm conviction that Mrs. Bruce was worthy to dwell with God. A childish idea possessed him that goodness of this genuine sort was pleasing to God, and that all that was necessary to get to heaven was to have enough of it. If he had read the Westminster Catechism, he might have learned how fallacious was this idea, and that many had gone to hell under its delusion.

But he was brought up not on a dismal catechismal diet, but upon Scriptural fare; and one of the first impressions he received from that book was that goodness was acceptable to God. If any learned divine had unkindly disturbed this well-founded confidence, and told him that Mrs. Bruce needed to borrow some righteousness to take her to heaven, he would have been puzzled to know where she was to find any that was better or more abundant than her own. It seemed to him that she had all she could hold, and that of the best quality.

Is this picture of that saintly life an idealization? Undoubtedly. But it is an ideal projected from a moral reality. And what better fruits can the purest human lives yield to us than that they awaken in us ideals of character which may be superior to their own attainments? The ideal, then, is but the transfiguration of the real. Every beautiful character furnishes its own halo. As I think of my ideal teacher and compare her with the actual, I am unable to distinguish one from the other. But I possess a firm conviction that, had I known this noble woman still better, I should have found her even more lovable in life than I am capable of painting her by any effort of my fancy.

Christianity has bequeathed to us, and Protestantism has jealously guarded from all rivalry, its grand ideal of the Perfect Man. Catholicism, with similar homage and even more tenderness, has unfolded the equally lofty vision of the Perfect Woman. I know of nothing which a Sunday-school can do so valuable for a child as to keep brightly burning before its eyes this dual vision of Perfection; and the best way to kindle it in the young heart is not by creeds, catechisms, or text-books, but by the illumining and inspiring influence of pure, holy, divine-human lives.

III.

THE SERMON GAUGE.

IS it owing to the enchantment of greater distance that the memories of the infant class seem brighter, more prismatic, than those of the regular Sunday-school department into which Asked-of-God was eventually ushered? Perhaps, as the boy grew, there were other things which excited his interest and stored the mind with honeyed recollections. But the difference may partly be accounted for in other ways. In the first place, the teacher of the infant class and the superintendent of the Sunday-school were as different as day is from night. The former was a noble, saintly woman; the latter was but a fraction of a man, and that fraction of indifferent quality. He failed to secure either the love or the respect of the scholars. His piety was nasal enough to be conventional, but was lacking in compass and resonance. He was a disciplinarian of the old school, fond of pulling the boys' ears; and as the boys had little or no fear of him, they took care that he should have abundant opportunity to practise his reformatory methods. He was a man of extremely small stature, and lacked the great soul which may invest the smallest frame with dignity and magnitude. On account of his diminutive stature, rather than with any reference to intemperate habits, he was known among the boys as "Beer Barrel." As his name began with B, this title formed with it an alliteration pleasing to a scornful ear. Boys are apt to be keen judges of human nature; and their instinct was justified in this case, for the superintendent, who was also a deacon in the church, suddenly disappeared one day, leaving a sorrow-cloud on the heart of his wife, and a deep sense of indignation in the minds of the community. The boys did not mourn his loss.

The teacher of the class was a humble, pious man, who had not the gift of teaching, but who, though not awakening love, commanded respect and esteem. The lessons, which were uniform throughout the school, soon became too dogmatic. It was like eating carobs to exchange the succulent food of Hebrew mythology for the husks of dogma which were given to us from week to week. "Scripture proofs" of various doctrines were printed on lesson papers, to be committed to memory; and once a month two or three "visitors" came, who, going the round of the classes, heard the scholars recite, individually, the verses they had learned. These verses were gathered from all parts of the Bible, and squeezed together into a kind of doctrinal pemmican, which was supposed to be concentrated nourishment for the youthful soul.

In those days — that is, about thirty years ago — the Sunday-school was held both morning and afternoon; and in the church above there was preaching three times a day. Remember that this was the regular Sunday diet of the congregation, and the regular Sunday labor of the minister. What would our congregations, who find it hard to get out to one service a day, say to three regular services, all of them of the same order, and all of them including a full-length sermon? And what would our ministers think of three sermons a week, besides an expository lecture on Tuesday evenings and a prayer-meeting on Friday? And here was the faithful Sunday-school teacher, who, if she attended, as she usually did, both sessions of the school and all the church services, had the luxury of five services every Sunday. The minister to-day may say that it would be as easy to preach three sermons of the kind that were deemed acceptable in those days as to prepare his one sermon, into which the accumulated thought of a whole week is poured. But this is only partially true, and only true of some men. There are ministers who have power of concentration, but not versatility. They find it easier to put all their thought into one topic than to spread it over three. They do not find it easy to get themes. It is the choice of a subject, and then the work of moulding it into a sermonic form, which troubles them, rather than the elaboration of a theme after it is chosen. Then there are men who do not know how to slight their work. A sermon represents a certain standard of excellence, and three sermons a week would mean to them a good sermon multiplied by three. While three weekly sermons must have been a terror to the indolent, it was upon the conscientious men, the workmen who did not wish to be ashamed, that the burden was heaviest. The fluent, easy writer or talker might toss off three sermons like mental soap-bubbles, filled with the inspiration of a good pair of lungs, and bursting into oblivion soon after delivery; but for the minister who disdained soap-bubbles, the hard-thinking, hard-writing man, whose thoughts oozed from the pen at a rate which could never be hurried, no matter how simple the theme, the three-sermon requisition must have been a treadmill grind. It was impossible for the average minister to preach so often without repeating himself. While he nominally preached one hundred and fifty sermons in a year, the new matter in them could be reduced to fifty, twenty-five, or a dozen. There was a magazine of theological and Scriptural phrases, and a large stock of well-worn platitudes upon which the minister could continually draw. The cut of the sermon might be the preacher's own, but the cloth was apt to be of second-hand material, a little threadbare in spots, and the garment did not always snugly fit the subject.

But we need not spend all our commiseration on the minister. The congregation deserves a generous share of our pity. Deluged with three sermons a Sunday, the second washing out the first, and the third washing out the second, what opportunity was there for the truth which every sermon should hold in solution to be gently precipitated in the soul of the hearer? The result of the operation was much like that of poor hydraulic mining, — a vast amount of water, a great deal of sand, and very little gold.

The reader must be warned, however, against accepting too confidently a boy's estimate of the value of those sermons. I am not disposed to accept it myself, for the reason that the sermons made little or no impression upon the boy's mind. Very likely the best things in these discourses were those which least stamped themselves upon his memory, and produced least effect upon his heart. To tell the truth, the boy found it necessary for his mental interest to have some other form of intellectual activity than that which a close attention to the sermon afforded. He was not expected to attend church three times a day, but was encouraged to be present both morning and afternoon; and his place in the church was not in the family pew, but in the gallery with the rest of the Sunday-school children. He never remembers to have disturbed the service in any way by restlessness or frivolity. His sympathies with the ministry were too early enlisted to permit him to offer any affront to the profession. He kept his foot in the house of God, but his mind wandered in a good many places where his feet were not permitted to go. From his position in the gallery, he could look down through the windows under the opposite gallery to the sidewalk below. There were three or four windows in the church commanded by his vision. As the church stood on a corner, one of these windows looked out upon a portion of the street on which the church faced, the others opened on the street at right angles to it. The passers-by were not numerous, but they alone gave life and interest to the street, the passage of a vehicle being extremely rare. The value of a sermon, at that time, Asked-of-God determined mainly by its length or brevity, a standard of judgment which many grown people still apply. By means of these windows, and the passers-by who could be seen from them, the boy mentally constructed a gauge for measuring the sermon and relieving the tedium of the delivery. As there are many older people who might wish to avail themselves of this invention, I will briefly describe it. Let the windows be marked, respectively, —

A, B, C.

As window A was on the corner, more pedestrians passed that point than any other. It was therefore made the basis of computation. Whenever five pedestrians passed A, a figure 1 was mentally carried to the credit of window B; when window B had five to its credit, one was passed to the credit of window C. It was a simple application of the multiplication table, made about the time the boy was furnishing his mind with that kind of upholstery. It was a form of geometrical progression, in which the progression of a given number of pedestrians was applied to the progression of a sermon. Letting x represent the sermon (as an unknown quantity and quality), the formula would be as follows: —

$$5\,a \times 5\,b \times c = x.$$

The numerical value of c expressed in pedestrians passing window A would be 25; that is, twenty-five persons would need to pass that window before window C would be credited with the unit which was supposed to be equal to the length of a sermon. The proportions observed in calculation may have varied from those given above, but the method was the same. The number of pedestrians required was generally fixed high enough to permit the sermon to be finished before the process of calculation was completed. A pleasing sense of disappointment was thus created in the child's mind entirely different from the sense of disappointment which the minister would have experienced had he known the effect or non-effect of his discourse on the youthful hearer.

Severe critics may be disposed to censure such forms of mental activity in church, amounting as it did to a systematic wandering from the sermon during its delivery. But, in defence of the child, it may be said that many ministers are themselves habitual wanderers in their discourses, and that they compel the respectfully attentive congregation to wander with them. The boy simply exercised his right to wander on his own account. And if we could go back to that congregation and look into the brains of those who were not asleep during these pulpit digressions, I have no doubt we should find that a large number of adult hearers were engaged in similar and perhaps less innocent excursions. To sleep in church is a practice conventionally disreputable, and those who are addicted to this vice may find some relief in the patent sermon gauge which I have described. The wide adoption of stained-glass windows renders the system less applicable to modern churches;

but, with the multiplication table as a basis, there are other devices which will suggest themselves.

The art of attention is one of the most valuable that can be acquired, and the boy afterward atoned somewhat for early delinquencies by beginning at the age of fourteen the practice of taking down the heads of every discourse he heard. Whole books were filled with the skeletons which were brought home from the Sunday sermon. In those days ministers took care to present the entire anatomy of their discourses to the congregation. It was of great help in making an abstract to have the preacher tell you when he got to thirdly and fourthly and fifthly, while under each of these numerical divisions two or three minor divisions were often grouped. To be sure, there was not always logical connection between the parts, but they served as stakes for the memory; and whenever there was a logical progression, it was easy to see it.

Of the sermons of those earliest years, only one made an impression on the memory so deep that it could not be effaced. "Cast thy bread upon the waters, for thou shalt find it after many days," was the text. The child's attention was at once arrested by the picture. Visions of loaves of bread cast into the East River came promptly before his mind. They would float down into the bay and come back again perhaps by some subsequent flood tide; but what would such water-soaked loaves be good for? Here was a text with a riddle in it. Eager interest awaited its solution.

The preacher painted a little picture, and it was all

plain. We could see the banks of the Nile, and the husbandman going forth to sow his seed in its overflowing waters. We could see the waters subside, and the seed germinating in the soil; and we could see, too, the abundant harvest which followed. The truth involved was inextricably blended with the illustration. There was no need of the sermon gauge that day. Who the preacher was or where he came from, I do not know. But his shadowy form is still visible, leaning slightly over the pulpit and telling that story. The next day, when the boy hearer went to a hardware store to make a purchase, he heard the porter telling his employer about this sermon, and the great impression it had made on his mind. Two birds at one shot, — a porter and a Sunday-school boy!

The preacher may or may not be in the land of the living; but one of his captured hearers has often wished that he might see his face once more, to cheer him with the assurance that he drove a truth into a boy's heart, and clinched it so firmly that it is there still.

IV.

THE TYPICAL MINISTER.

DR. DEWEY, in his Autobiography, gives us a mental photograph, taken vividly on a childish brain, of the first pastor he recalls: "To the recollections of my childhood, this old pastor presents a very distinct and I may say somewhat portentous figure, — tall, large-limbed, pale, ghostly almost, with slow movement and hollow tone, with eyes dreamy and kindly, I believe, but spectral to me, — coming into the house with a heavy, deliberate, and solemn step, making me feel as if the very chairs and tables were conscious of his presence and did him reverence; and when he stretched out his long, bony arm, and said, 'Come here, child,' I felt something as if a spiritualized ogre had invited me. Nevertheless, he was a man, I believe, of a very affectionate and tender nature: indeed, I afterward came to think so; but at that time, and up to the age of twelve, it is a strict truth that I did not regard Mr. Judson as properly a human being, — as a *man* at all. If he had descended from the planet Jupiter, he could not have been a bit more preternatural and strange to me."

Dr. Dewey's minister was not an exceptional figure, but a typical one. The ministerial cloth, in those days, was woven on one loom, and cut after one fashion. It is not probable that men were born any nearer alike than they are now; yet the *average* ministers of that day seemed as much alike as the candles in a box. There were some of larger girth than others, standing in more prominent candlesticks and casting a more brilliant light; but the conventional ministers all seemed to be made out of the same tallow, and most of them were cast in the same mould. I say *conventional* ministers, because we do find among them ministers who were not conventional, — ministers whose broad humanity ripped the seams of the clerical vesture, — ministers who, so to speak, burst off the regulation Sunday-go-to-meeting buttons, and appeared ecclesiastically out at the elbows, because too large for the system which confined them. Volcanic individuality will not easily be repressed; and there is nothing more interesting for the biographical spectator than to observe, now and then, a ministerial Vesuvius breaking forth with eccentric and brilliant eruptions of genius in the midst of this battalion of candles. Memorials of originality, strength, and even grotesqueness of character, appear among our pulpit annals. Nevertheless, if we seek the typical minister of fifty or sixty years ago, we must go to the candle box. The theological system under which he was reared, the prevalent ideal of ministerial life, combined with a heritage of professional precedents, all helped to mould him.

Perhaps the accepted idea of *other-worldliness* had as much to do in shaping his character as anything else, and it was this idea which he constantly reflected. The minister was the shadow of a coming event; he stood not for time, but for eternity. This world was but a highway to the next; he could not tarry by the way. The minister was an adverb of place; "Heaven" was written on his forehead. Perhaps spirituality may be popularly considered his distinguishing attitude; but ghostliness, I think, would be a better term. He was a professional spectre, moving like a shadowy warning among the haunts of men, now pointing his finger to a zone above, now pointing it with still more solemn warning to a zone below. Dr. Dewey describes him as "strange and preternatural;" and the impression he made on his boyish mind was that he was not properly a human being, — was not a *man* at all.

This type of minister, though rapidly disappearing, was very familiar thirty years ago, and made its impression on a boyhood less remote than the date of Dr. Dewey's.

The first minister who left a picture — dim and distantly vague though it be — upon the writer's mind was not of this class. As casually noted on a previous page, he was not only a minister, but a practising physician, who gave his time during the week to his patients, and on Sunday broke the bread of life to the little band of Christians who assembled with apostolic simplicity in an upper room. Perhaps it was the affectionate interest and tender-sympathy which Jesus showed for the physical ills of humanity, his power of healing the body as well as the soul, his interest in the life the people lived, which relieved him of all appearance of professional priestliness. In the same gracious way did Dr. Barker combine the office of the good physician with that of the bishop of souls. His duties as a doctor relieved him from the professional exclusiveness of the minister. He had a direct and immediate relation to this world. His title as "doctor" suggested solely his healing office, and a very intimate relation to the laity, while the same title applied to the minister only heightened his professional character, the doctor of divinity being a *sublimated* ghost, or a ghost saturated with theology. The minister is often invoked to dismiss the soul with his blessing at the exit of life; but Dr. Barker was also present at its entrance, and ushered into this world with benedictory skill enough children to form a populous infant class. They were never to my knowledge gathered together under one roof, for his surgical practice exceeded his pastoral in extent; but he found his lambs scattered here and there in different sheepfolds, and had a shepherd's love for them all. As he came on spiritual missions as well as medical ones, and interwove his parish calls with his professional visits, the appearance of his horse and chaise at the door awakened no unnecessary alarm. Asked-of-God welcomed its arrival, for there was a prospect that he would get a ride when it left.

Of the multitude of sights and sounds that patter on the childish brain, the surest to make a permanent indentation is some voice or aspect, some gracious ministry of love. The children whom Jesus blessed so tenderly, if old enough to receive any impressions of life whatever, probably never forgot the man who took them into his arms and caressed them. So Asked-of-God finds in a dim corner of his mental picture-gallery a miniature, framed in a golden halo, of a man with a godlike face, tenderly placing his hand upon a little child's head and smiling a fatherly blessing.

The vision of this large-hearted, genial man, who might appropriately have been called the doctor-shepherd, gives place a few years later to the ministerial spectre, "the ghost in spite of himself." Of his preaching not a shred or atom is recalled; but his pastoral visitations were youthfully classified with the measles, the whooping-cough, and other visitations of a distressing sort. Nothing harsh or unkind is ever associated with his memory: he was not a boy-hater, a scold, a disciplinarian. It would have been a relief to think of him as having some of these attributes of humanity. His very virtues helped to make him *un*-human. He was a minister, not a man. The boy regarded him as the embodiment of irreproachable and unapproachable saintliness. His smile and his words were uniformly pleasant, but they seemed to be the expression of his professional goodness.

This man was fitted for heaven, and heaven seemed the place best fitted for him. He belonged to a totally different sphere of life from that in which a young boy is accustomed to rejoice. If his solemn dignity could have kindly suffered an occasional lapse,—if the boy could have seen him riding on an omnibus, or chasing his hat in a gust of wind, or carrying home a fish for dinner, or doing a hundred things which a country minister might do without reproach, — confidence in his sympathetic humanity would have been restored. But the conventionalities of city life perfectly insulated him in the proprieties of his profession. To the city boy at least, who saw him only in the pulpit and in his parish calls, he was ever and always a minister.

The memory of these calls is not abundant, for the reason that the boy generally took care to be away from home when they occurred. The moment the minister was spied on the street in the vicinity of No. 32, the location of one young resident was swiftly changed. The home of a little Catholic boy next door was naturally deemed safe from invasion. Catholicism thus furnished an asylum for a self-exiled refugee from the oppression of Protestant priestcraft. On one occasion, however, the vigilance of the oppressed had become unsuspectingly lax. The minister was already at the gate before his presence was discovered. The fence which divided the besieged home from the Catholic protectory was too high for the refugee to scale. The wood-house, which would have furnished concealment, must have been locked. The only resource left was to rush upstairs, alarm the house, and accept such concealment as circumstances afforded. A bedroom off the sitting-room furnished a temporary haven. Crawling far under the bed, the refugee felt safe from detection, albeit his position was not a very comfortable one. The voices in the adjoining room could be plainly heard. The advent of the ministerial tone was clearly audible. The hum of conversation was varied by no light or lively strains, but presently the monotone became more solemn and measured. The youthful prisoner knew what that meant: his mother had asked her pastor to read the Bible. A profound reverence for that book forbade the listener to object to the quality of anything chosen from between its lids; but it cannot be denied that, under certain circumstances, some of its chapters are rather long. Whether from reverence for the pauses of the book, or because a divine intention was presumed in the length of the chapters, the minister of that day seldom began a chapter without feeling a conscientious obligation to finish it. Finally, there was a brief pause and a shifting of the chairs, and then the solemn, dirge-like tone began again. The practised ear of the fugitive knew what that meant: the minister had begun to pray. There was little that was cheerful in the situation of the stow-away during the long and dreary minutes that followed. His position was a constrained and humiliating one. He longed more than ever for the Catholic protectory over the fence; and it is reasonably safe to assume that he made a fresh resolution, under the inspiration of the minister's prayer, — and that was never to be blockaded in this way again, if he could help it. The minister of that period invariably prayed for each individual member of the household when he knelt at the family altar. The youthful culprit has since wondered what kind of a blessing the minister would have asked upon his guilty head if he had known that the pastoral advent had driven him under a bed in the next room.

In the march of events the conventional, ghostly, otherworldly ministerial spectre is passing away. The pressure of the present life, with its multifarious obligations, its temptations, difficulties, burdens, sorrows, and perils, is engaging more than ever the thought and labor of the pulpit. Sermons are more practical, and have a direct bearing upon the ordinary relations of life. Professional etiquette is less exacting. The minister can come down during the week from his pulpit stilts. People can meet him without thinking of a graveyard. He is learning to talk in his natural tones, and by and by may learn to preach in a tone as natural as that in which he talks.

V.

REVIVAL FIRES.

THERE is a third meeting-house in New York to which the reader's attention is invited. It has long since been transformed into a public school; only the shell of the original building is left. Its surroundings are prosaic and uninviting; but, for the writer, it is nevertheless invested with the sanctity of precious and holy memories. It is not from time, place, or circumstance that the soul builds its shrines, but from the rich and sacred material of its most hallowed experiences. How illy the rude meeting-houses of the first New England settlers compared with the magnificent cathedrals they had left behind! But the idea of liberty and conscience which they carried to the little meeting-house was larger than the cathedral they had abandoned. The wilderness was a highway unto God, and their very deprivations furnished fuel for piety.

Homely and humble was the third city meeting-house which Asked-of-God began to attend just as he was crossing the threshold of his teens. The church and Sunday-school to which he had gone during the first decade of his life had committed ecclesiastical suicide. It was, as has been said, born of a quarrel, had lived through several years of peace and semi-prosperity, but finally put the knife of dissension to its own throat, and suffered rapid dissolution. The elements of which it was composed attached themselves to other organizations. Asked-of-God and his mother went to the church from which the disbanded society had originally seceded.

A cold state of spiritual torpor had come over the old church. There was languor in the pulpit, languor in the pew; the prayer-meetings were held in the latitude of the North Pole; the Sunday-school had gone into a state of hibernation. The church, taken as a whole, was little more than a religious dormitory. Occasionally a meteor flashed in the pulpit for a Sunday or two, or somebody with a gong-like voice bombarded the sealed ears with brazen warnings. Then the people opened their eyes, looked around, confessed in prayer-meeting their "leanness of spirit," prayed conventionally to be thawed out, and then dropped off for another six months' nap. Two or three short and sterile pastorates followed by a long interregnum had scattered the flock and reduced what was left to a state of comparative inanition.

It was at this critical stage in the life of the church that a young minister suddenly appeared with a load of revival kindling-wood and a flaming torch in his hand. His earnestness was intense, his eloquence magnetic. He was but twenty-eight years of age, had not received the disadvantage — as it seemed to some of the people — of a college education, but had seen a great deal of life, and was possessed of a strong pair of lungs which served to blow his ardent discourses into roaring, leaping flames of speech like a prairie fire driven by a tornado.

It was a pleasing experience for the church and congregation to have a live coal on the altar. Enough interest was developed to give the young minister a call. He promptly accepted, and immediately set to work to rouse the church from its lethargy. He began with the deacons, whose religion, if not frozen so hard as that of some of the younger and more worldly members, was yet so thoroughly congealed that they could bear a heavy weight of pulpit appeal without slumping. When the deacons thawed out, the church began to thaw out, and the prayer-meeting became a freshet of penitential confession. The pastor preached a powerful sermon on the necessity of breaking up the fallow ground of the heart, and another from the text, "The backslider in heart shall be filled with his own ways." The church was fairly roused. It began to see the peril of lost souls. It girded itself anew to work for their salvation.

Having melted and warmed the heart of the church, the pastor turned his artillery upon the redoubts of Satan. With blazing earnestness, he exhorted sinners to flee from the wrath to come. Originality of thought, logical power, and literary grace were qualities of style to which he did not lay claim, and which might have impeded the force of his direct and cogent appeals. But he had great dramatic power, an active imagination, and could use rhetorical color with much effect in painting the terrible condition of the lost. It was not by appeals to the conscience or to the heart that he produced "conviction." The unregenerate "moral man" and the unregenerate sinner were both in the same category. They were equally in danger. It was his mission to declare to men the fact assured by revelation, — that in the sin of Adam condemnation had fallen upon the whole human race; that all had sinned and come short of the glory of God. He who sinned in one point was guilty of all. It was the office of the minister to awaken men, through the blessing of the Holy Spirit, to a sense of their utterly lost and undone condition, and to point out to them the only way of escape, through the blood of a crucified Redeemer. The preacher presented, with all the power he could command, the terrors of the law. His sermons were full of the smoke and thunder of Sinai. He "uncovered the pit of hell," — it was a favorite expression, — and described, after the manner of Jonathan Edwards, the endless agonies of those committed to its tortures.

Was it at all strange that, after hearing a few of these sermons, the mind of the boy became actively "awakened" concerning his own salvation? He had been taught by his mother that God is Love; and for children who have not reached years of responsibility, that is generally the way in which Baptists picture him. They have never harbored the cruel dogma of infant damnation. But now that he had reached his teens, God was presented to him in the aspect of unrelenting Justice. He was called upon to consider a wholly new set of premises. These premises were the fall of Adam, the consequent condemnation of the entire race, salvation only through belief on Jesus Christ, who had shed his blood as a ransom for sinners.

The youth never thought of doubting these premises. Were they not recorded in God's infallible Word? Did not the pastor, the deacons, — in fact, Christians everywhere, — believe them? The pastor stood on the walls of Zion as an ambassador to lost souls, proclaiming a message of peace and pardon to the repentant and of everlasting torture to the obdurate.

The youth was not unmoved by these appeals. He was forced to hold an inquest on the condition of his own soul. That inquest disclosed the fact that he was a sinner. His memory was hung with pictures of transgression. They were small pictures, and not flagrantly vicious. He had never taken anything that did not belong to him, had never to his knowledge wilfully told a lie, and had only rarely caught himself humming a secular tune on "the Sabbath day." He was not in the habit of swearing. Only once in his young life had he used the word "damn," and that was under extenuating circumstances. And yet he knew that the word had been recorded in heaven; for should we not at the judgment day give account of every idle word that we had spoken? Had he not *thought* " damn," too, a good many times when he had not said it? Had he not been guilty of murdering his brother with angry thoughts? Had he not said, "Thou fool," and thus incurred the danger of hell fire? Any one of these sins was enough to condemn him to everlasting punishment, — not because they were so wicked in themselves, but because they were violations of God's holy laws, and because they disclosed the evil heart of wickedness and unbelief that reigned within the youthful bosom.

But this was not all. Even if his conscience could have given him a clean bill of release from incurred penalty, it would not suffice. He was a child of Adam, the representative of the race. He shared the consequences of his guilt. Nothing but a complete change of heart through the influence of the Holy Spirit and the impartation of a new spiritual nature could remove the original stain, and nothing but Christ's blood could remove the condemnation with which this original and acquired guilt would be visited. What was that condemnation? An active imagination painted it in lurid colors before his eyes: a burning lake of fire and brimstone, everlastingly unquenchable, peopled with devils whose eternal occupation was to augment the tortures of the damned. The dramatic intensity with which the minister described the judgment day is not yet forgotten; the sublime convulsions which rent the world, the unveiling of the awful judgment seat, the gathering of the nations, the resurrection of the dead at the sound of the archangel's trump, and the final separation of the righteous (which meant believers in the righteousness of Christ) from the ungodly. It was this thought of eternal separation from his mother, sister, and friends that made the future "out of Christ" seem terribly dark and distressing.

The lad had never harbored any hatred to his Maker. His thought of God had always been sweet, loving, tender. But now he had learned that God was angry with the wicked every day, and that he, as a descendant of Adam, had incurred his wrath. God might wish to be forgiving, but his justice would not allow him. The full price of guilt must be paid. But there was one way in which the love of God still shone through the clouds of his anger; it was in sending his beloved Son into the world, that whosoever believed on him might not perish, but have everlasting life.

Is it a wonder that, with these threatenings hanging over his head and with this way of escape provided, the youth should have been moved to insure his future happiness? Convicted of sin and guilt, why should he not fly to the fountain for uncleanness? He was seeking reconciliation with God; should he not seize the olive branch? Peace had departed from his soul; where should he find it but in Christ?

Asked-of-God determined to go to the inquiry meeting.

VI.

FINDING PEACE.

THE name "inquiry meeting" may need a little explanation for some of my readers. The inquiry meeting is a method instituted by the revival preacher to ascertain how much game he has brought down with his fowling-piece. It is a kind of dynameter by which he tests the power of his preaching. More aptly figured, it is the minister's clinique, a dispensary for sin-sick souls to receive the balm and tonic of the gospel. The first object of the revival preacher is to make sinners uncomfortable. It is the object of the inquiry meeting to restore to them an assured peace. After each sermon it is customary for the minister to appoint an hour and place at which those who have been convicted of sin may meet him. It is thus necessary for the convicted soul to take the initiative. But in well-organized revivals the minister has a corps of keen assistants throughout the congregation, who are swift to detect the slightest symptom of conviction, and to urge the sinner to take prompt steps for its relief. When the whole church is warmed up, then each member becomes an active agent for bringing in fresh fuel for the revival flame. Strong and direct personal solicitation on the part of friends who are laboring under "the burden of souls" often has much to do in filling the inquiry room. Here the symptoms are carefully examined by the preacher, who questions the patient with that searching professional curiosity with which a doctor sometimes examines an invalid. Theological pathology differs, however, from medical pathology in this respect, — that the soul-leech often seeks to make his patient feel that he is really worse than is actually the case. We have indeed seen doctors of this sort, but they always create a suspicion of quackery. The theological healer assumes, however, that the first and most important thing is to awaken the conscience of his patient to an alarming sense of his danger. The presumption is, that the deeper and more incisive the consciousness of sin, the more grateful will the sinner be for the cure that is effected.

It was one clear, cool October night that Asked-of-God found himself standing at the foot of the narrow staircase that led to the minister's study in the church, where the inquiry meeting was held. The meeting was held in the evening, to give an opportunity to those who could not go in the day. To the boy the hour was a grateful one; for, like Nicodemus, it gave him an opportunity to go under cover of the darkness. He had taken this step entirely alone. No pressure had been brought to bear upon him, except that exerted in the pulpit. No one had spoken to him personally in regard to his soul; but he had learned that he had one, and the great question which agitated him was, what should it profit him if he gained the whole world and lost his own soul.

There was a moment of indecision, as he stood at the foot of the stairs. The stars were shining peacefully above; there was no sign without that the world was at enmity with God; yet he looked up, and thought of the time when these heavens should roll away as a parched scroll. A severe struggle followed between timidity and resolution. Finally, he opened the lower door and went softly up the stairs, his heart beating like a little trip-hammer. He paused a moment at the top, then, with a final and determined effort, knocked at the door. The door opened. The little room was filled with converts and their friends, and all eyes were turned on the young and bashful Nicodemus. The pastor welcomed him, and gave him a seat. He then proceeded with the examination of several of the candidates. The youthful inquirer had time to collect himself. It seemed to him, then and there, as though a great burden had been rolled off his soul. He had taken the first step, it was easy to take the rest. It seemed to him now as if he had brought himself into alliance with the people of God. He felt that he could "accept Jesus;" he knew that Jesus would accept him. He was perfectly familiar with the theoretical plan of salvation. He could answer intellectually any questions likely to be presented. He had not learned to distinguish entirely his emotional from his intellectual states. Some of the converts answered glibly enough. Some had found peace; others were still in doubt and despair. But there was one candidate whose perfect sincerity made a profound impression upon him. The minister asked him a question.

The candidate hesitated, and after a period of silence said, "I know the intellectual answer you want, but I wish to be sure that I feel so before answering your question."

I have forgotten just what questions were put; still more have I forgotten the stammering answers which were made. But there was a statement of the consciousness of sin and the penalty it involved, and the consciousness of pardon and the joy it brought. The transition from the state of condemnation to that of peace and happiness was a simple and easy one for the boy to make. He was not dissolved into tears, like some of the candidates who cried in the agony of their grief over their lost and undone condition. He recalls vividly the figure of a woman, who for several days gave way to these penitential paroxysms. She seemed to be on the brink of despair. And one of the first things that Asked-of-God did after his conversion was to go with a few young converts to her house and pray that the burden might be rolled from her soul, as Christian dropped it at the wicket gate. He could not easily see why, if one felt his lost state, he could not as promptly accept the remedy which was offered. He was sometimes, however, led to doubt his own conversion, because it was not of the startling kind. The minister seemed to be better satisfied when a perfect "law work" was executed in the soul, when a convert had cowered under the smoke and thunder of Sinai or been smitten on the way from Jerusalem to Damascus.

A few days after attendance on the inquiry meeting, the young candidate was visited by the minister and one of the deacons. A second ordeal came when, after being accepted by them, he had to stand up with a few others on the Friday-night meeting, and "relate his experience." One of his companions on that occasion was a sailor who had led a hard and intemperate life. To those who knew what he had been, the story of his conversion made a great impression. Most of the converts made their narration of experience as dramatic as possible. There was an endeavor to fix the precise time when they were convicted of sin, and the precise time when they were relieved of it. There was a disposition to discover something almost miraculous in their experience. Some of the most simple events were magnified into supernatural interpositions. But Asked-of-God had nothing miraculous, nothing dramatic to relate. The transition seemed a natural and an easy one. Peace seemed to come to him when he ascended the stairs into the pastor's study, and the door he opened there seemed to admit him into a larger and more joyful life. This was about as exactly as he could fix the chronology of his conversion. For some weeks it was a matter of regret to him that he had not had some more revolutionary and tempestuous experience. But he afterward found great satisfaction in reading Jacob Abbott's "Young Christian," especially in learning that it is not absolutely necessary to hate God before one can love him, and that a conversion which was as silent and undemonstrative as the growth of a plant might be as genuine as one which seemed to be a striking miracle of Divine grace. When, after relating his experience,

Asked-of-God and the other candidates retired to another room to await the verdict of the church, the boy's mother was asked if she had seen any great change in him. She was obliged to reply that she had not; he had always been an obedient son. The examination, however, was satisfactory, the candidate was admitted, and the following Sunday night was appointed for the baptism.

VII.

THE BAPTISM.

BAPTISTS have suffered much from misrepresentation concerning the ordinance from which they receive their name, and upon which it may be readily conceded they place undue emphasis. A common form of misrepresentation is seen in the statement so often made by people of other evangelical denominations that Baptists consider baptism as "a saving ordinance." All the Baptist blood (and water) in my veins rises in protest against such misstatements. On the contrary, it is probable that no branch of the Christian Church has done more to uproot a superstitious belief in the pernicious doctrine of baptismal regeneration than the Baptists. It is just here that a sharp line has divided them from Romanists, Lutherans, and old-time Episcopalians. The Romanist believes that unless baptismal water is applied to the infant, the curse of original sin is not removed, and the child is eternally lost. Luther held the same doctrine. Article IX. of the Augsburg Confession expressly condemned Anabaptists who affirmed "that children are saved without baptism." And the article is still taught, though with less harshness, by Lutherans to-day. The Baptists, on the other hand, have persistently denied that baptism effects regeneration, or that it secures in any way the salvation of either infant or adult. Baptism has never been used by them as a talisman, as a ticket to heaven. They have refused to administer it except to believers, those who they assume have consciously been convicted of sin and experienced a change of heart. While Calvinists, Romanists, and Lutherans alike have held to the doctrine that millions on millions of helpless infants have been consigned to perdition, Baptists have maintained the salvability of infants, and have always protested against the pagan notion that the application of water in any quantity, little or great, could open the gates of heaven.

As to the way of salvation, Baptists find it not in water, but in blood. They accept the vicarious view of the atonement of Jesus; and no evangelical denomination preaches with more constancy and power the doctrine that men must accept and believe on a crucified Saviour, and obtain redemption through his blood.

What, then, is the significance of the act of baptism to the Baptist? It is simply an evidence of obedience to the Master. Jesus himself, at mature age, accepted this form of consecration, and prescribed it for his disciples. The Baptist feels that he is following in his Master's footsteps. It is not a doorway to heaven, but a doorway to the church. By this act he enters into fellowship with Jesus, and fellowship with his disciples. Baptism to him is not a sign of the covenant; it has nothing to do with the Hebrew rite of circumcision; it is a purely Christian institution, and has a symbolism clearly its own.

THE BAPTISM. 57

If Baptists are to be criticised with reference to their observance of this ordinance, it is not for believing in its salvatory character, but for holding with such unyielding tenacity to immersion as the only legitimate form of the service, and refusing to regard those who have adopted either pouring or sprinkling as baptized Christians. The spiritual significance of this service, the consecration it expresses, should be esteemed of far more importance than the quantity of water employed or the method of its application. At the same time the writer must confess that, perhaps owing to the form of his education, the service loses most of its symbolic force when in adult baptism sprinkling is substituted for immersion.

Apart from the necessity they urge of following the example of Jesus as closely as possible, Baptists find the symbolism of immersion expressed by Paul in Romans vi. 4, 5: "We were buried therefore with him through baptism into death: that, like as Christ was raised from the dead through the glory of the Father, so we also might walk in newness of life. For if we have become united with him by the likeness of his death, we shall also be by the likeness of his resurrection." Immersion is a burial and a resurrection. It expresses the death of the "old man," the body of sin, and the rising to a new life. It does not produce regeneration, but it appropriately figures it. Sprinkling, on the other hand, conveys no such suggestion: it is rather a covenant seal on the forehead, figuring a totally different idea, devoid of the poetry, as also of the inconvenience and discomfort, of immersion. In immersion, it is necessary that the candidate be entirely buried under the water. The writer once saw a baptismal service repeated because the candidate's face was not wholly covered. The second time, he was put a foot beneath the surface to make sure of completely burying a somewhat prominent nose. In sprinkling, however, a drop of water suffices; and the case of excessive submersion noted above may be paralleled by a case of sprinkling in which the minister found that the font, through the neglect of the sexton, was entirely dry. He went on with the service, however, just as if it were full, and gave the baby a dry baptism; and the parents, and we presume the baby, were quite as well satisfied as if it had been a deluge.

The writer has been surprised from time to time to learn how many there are who have never seen an immersion in the religious sense of the word. Non-Baptist friends who have witnessed the ceremony have confessed to the writer that they found it more amusing than impressive. It must be owned that in its administration there is but a step between the sublime and the ridiculous. But all ritualistic services depend much for their impression upon the associations they awaken. A Roman Catholic service may be a tedious mummery to a Protestant, as a Protestant service may seem barren and prosaic to a Catholic. It is wholly due to education and association, perhaps, that baptism by immersion always seems to the writer, when decorously administered, a profoundly impressive service. To be sure, it is often made the subject of innocent pleasantry and sometimes of poor and reprehensible jokes. Baptists themselves must be held responsible for much of this good and bad wit. I have heard as much joking on the subject of baptism in social life among Baptists as anywhere else. .And on occasions of Union meetings, anniversaries, and public gatherings where Baptists and Pedobaptists have met in friendly relationship, the subject of baptism could always be relied upon to furnish most of the jokes for the occasion. This hydrous wit, we believe, is growing less common, simply because the possibilities of banter on both sides are wellnigh exhausted.

The writer confesses, however, that there is one form of the service which acts on him very much as a red rag acts on a bull. It is when in the dead of winter a hole is cut in the ice on a pond or river, to which the candidate is driven and immersed. Such was the experience of the writer's mother when a young girl. He hesitates to say how many miles she rode in an omnibus with others on a' cold winter day to the scene of this baptismal desecration, or how far she was compelled to ride after the service in wet garments. Such a violation of physiological law is not only foolish, it is criminal, and deserves to be impaled on every lance of wit or irony which can expose its palpable and inexcusable absurdity. Ministers who perform such baptisms should be liable to indictment for manslaughter. Baptists who feel bound to follow Jesus to the very letter ought to know that the practice of submersion in icebound streams is just as unscriptural as pouring or sprinkling. If anything is certain, it is that Jesus was not baptized in that way.

But no one who views the ordinance of baptism as a spectator only can form any idea of its significance to the young convert whose heart is aflame with love and gratitude to his Saviour, and who rejoices to follow his distinct and positive command. To robust men and boys, who are fairly accustomed to the water, the service presents no element of fear; but to weak and timid women, who have not had the preliminary training furnished by the swimming bath, baptism by immersion is a severe test of courage. The probability of drowning is a very remote one, especially when the service is performed in a church baptistery; but the natural aversion to submersion in cold water is something which neither reason nor theology can overcome, and it often costs the female candidate a hard struggle to submit to the ceremony. On the other hand, just as Hindu women, under the excitement of religious exaltation and the impulse of a strong if mistaken sense of duty, could cast themselves upon the funeral pyre, so it is often remarkable to see the beautiful composure, cheerful courage, and even joyful enthusiasm with which women naturally hydrophobic will go to baptism, when gratitude and love for Jesus impel them.

Asked-of-God had made "a public profession of his faith" on Friday night; the baptism was fixed for the following Sunday evening. The interval to the young candidate was a period of indescribable religious exaltation. There is no joy so intense as that which comes through the free, unbounded exercise of the religious sentiment, whatever may be the object which is invested with the glow of its emotion.

THE BAPTISM.

The baptismal Sunday was a bright October day. It seemed to the young convert unlike any other Sunday he had ever lived. All Nature, or as much of it as gets into such a city as New York, was invested with a preternatural charm. As he looked up to the sky that morning, it seemed as if the heavens must part and the dove descend, — a vision which may come to those who are baptized in the river, but which is less natural for those who, like Asked-of-God, are baptized in the evening in a church tank. The morning services, instead of being irksome to him as before, were listened to with delight. The Sunday-school had a new interest. But the climax of the day was the evening hour. A half-hour before the service he ascended once more, though this time without trepidation, the stairs leading to the pastor's study, which, on baptismal occasions, was used as a dressing-room for the male converts, a room on the opposite side of the church being reserved for the women. Both were immediately behind the pulpit. It is customary for each new convert to be assisted by one or more friends. A change of clothes was taken to the church. A robe of suitable length, and properly weighted at the bottom to keep it from floating on the water, was selected and put on. The candidates then entered the church, and took seats in the front pew reserved for them.

The church was crowded to excess. Baptism is a dramatic service. It generally draws a good house. The best seats are in the gallery near the baptistery; and for these people would wait for an hour before the service, and then scamper for the front rows like boys at a circus when the doors were opened.

The sermon was one of great power, from a Baptist standpoint. It was on the cities of refuge. They were supposed to be typical of the refuge afforded by Christ to the sinner. The preacher drew a vivid picture of the shedder of blood fleeing for his life to the city of refuge, hotly pursued by the avenger. He exhorted those out of Christ to fly to this refuge from the wrath to come. The sermon was given without notes, was delivered with great earnestness, and was instrumental in ultimately bringing to the baptismal waters some who came merely as spectators.

At the conclusion of the sermon, the pastor gave out a hymn, which, if I mistake not, was,

> "In all my Lord's appointed ways,
> My journey I'll pursue."

The pulpit was removed from the platform, the carpet rolled back, the flooring taken up, and the baptistery disclosed, during which time the pastor had exchanged his preaching suit for a baptismal robe. Returning, he offered a short prayer on the perilously narrow strip of platform which was left. The candidates then ascended the stairs to the platform, and descended one by one into the pool, and were successively baptized. It is customary for some ministers to ask the convert as he stands in the water, "Dost thou believe on the Lord Jesus Christ with all thy heart?" but, more generally, the statement of experience he has made to the church is deemed sufficient; and the formula then is, "Upon public profession of thy faith, I baptize thee in the name of the Father and of the Son and of the Holy Ghost. Amen." At the word "Amen," the candidate is theoretically supposed to hold his breath, while the minister gently dips him beneath "the liquid wave," as the standing water in the tank is sometimes poetically called. On coming up, his face is wiped by the minister with a handkerchief previously furnished him; and he passes as soon as possible to the dressing-room, the choir singing a "Hallelujah" or a verse from some hymn.

The water had been warmed by means of coils of pipes passing round a stove, so that the temperature was not uncomfortable. But from a failure to hold his breath at the proper moment, Asked-of-God drew a small quantity of water into his windpipe, which nearly strangled him. But he would have been perfectly willing to be strangled that night, if the glory of God had required it. He was permitted, however, to make a humbler and a less tragic sacrifice. Retiring to the dressing-room and changing his clothes for a dry suit, he found it impossible to get on his boots. Soap, the only persuasive available, was tried without success. Stamping, jerking, and beating did no good. After fifteen minutes of unavailing effort, he was obliged to abandon the attempt; and, taking his boots under his arm, the young disciple humbly ran home barefooted, far happier than if he had ridden there with a coach and four.

VIII.

A BUSY CONVERT.

THE formalities of admission to the Baptist church are not complicated. Asked-of-God had attended the inquiry meeting, had related his experience, had been baptized. The only ceremony that followed was the extension of the right hand of fellowship by the pastor to the new converts. This was done at the communion service, which was held on the first Sunday in every month. When the convert received the hand of fellowship, it was commonly said that he was " taken in." Worldly and irreverent wits sometimes said that this was precisely the term to apply to it. As converts were baptized nearly every Sunday evening during the revival, the crop in the course of the month was a large one. Sometimes thirty or forty were received at the communion service. It was something of a tax upon the pastor, after a few general remarks, to take each convert by the hand, and say a word which applied especially to his case; and the youth thought that, as a minister, he would much rather baptize the candidates than "take them in" afterwards. Indeed, the imitation of baptism by immersion was always included when as a child he had played church with his little sister.

A BUSY CONVERT.

Without signing any creed or covenant whatever, but simply by public profession and baptism, Asked-of-God found himself ushered into all the privileges and duties of a church-member at the tender age of fourteen. Whether or not he had given his heart to the Lord, he had certainly committed it pretty fully to the church. Apart from the affectionate interest that centred in the home, all his other interests at this time were centred here. It was also the religious life of the church which furnished the chief attraction. With three or four meetings on Sunday, and meetings during the revival season every night in the week, there was no time for other engagements. The church itself furnished no social life except that which was incidental to its religious meetings. Coming together every night in the week, the members naturally saw a great deal of each other. But it was not principally the social bond which held them together. No amusements, or entertainments, or receptions of any kind were furnished by the church. Private theatricals, operettas, or dances would not have been tolerated for a moment; but, beyond this, there was no " Young People's Society " for intellectual and moral improvement, no " Benevolent Society," no social club of any kind. Not even, as I remember, was there that usual and generally indispensable luxury of an American church, a sewing-society. If there were, it was confined to a small circle of ladies, and was not used as a lever for social purposes. The object of the church, under the earnest lead of its pastor, was not to educate, gratify, or amuse, but simply to save souls.

The only interruption of this unvarying solemnity of meetings and services occurred once a year, when the anniversary of the Sunday-school was held in the church, the children "speaking pieces," singing, and conducting dialogues, to the great delight of the mothers and fathers and other interested spectators who thronged the house. A repetition of the anniversary was always necessary to accommodate those who failed to get in the first time. This was the nearest approach to the theatre that Asked-of-God ever attended, until he had nearly reached the age of manhood, with the exception of a single visit to Mr. Barnum's pious lecture-room at the old Museum, corner of Broadway and Ann Streets. This occurred before the boy's conversion, and was appropriately punished by a fit of nausea which culminated in a Broadway omnibus.

Antipathy to dramatic performances of any kind was so strong in the church that when a young convert whose fervor had cooled a few months after his baptism was known to have visited a theatre, he was promptly admonished, and on a repetition of the offence was expelled. This severity of discipline may have been sharpened by the consciousness that the church had been guilty of graduating a professional actor from one of its Sunday-school exhibitions. A few years previous to this revival season, and under a different pastorate, an anniversary was held which was prepared with great elaboration. A representation of the bondage of the Israelites in Egypt, their deliverance by Moses, the rage and pursuit of Pharaoh, was attempted on a large scale. No scenery was used; but, by means of dialogue and costume, an effect quite unusual for such an occasion was produced. To the son of the pastor, a talented young man on the verge of manhood, was assigned the rôle of Pharaoh. He appeared on the stage, which occupied the place of the pulpit, arrayed in royal garments of scarlet and gold of the most brilliant description, and with a crown and sceptre of equal magnificence. Moses, represented by a meek and lovable young man, was wrapped in flowing white robes; and the Israelites and Egyptians were provided with Oriental costumes furnished by a well-known panorama company. It would of course have been "wicked" to use costumes which had been defiled by unholy representatives on the stage. The pastor's son was possessed of considerable dramatic ability for one without training; and his representation of the rage of Pharaoh at the departure of the Israelites, when, "amazed, ashamed, and confounded to the dust," he tore a passion to tatters, was very effective in contrast to the meek and placid demeanor of the white-robed Moses. The exhibition drew an immense house, and was profitable from a pecuniary point of view.

The use of the costumes, however, and the spirited acting which accompanied them, called forth much comment from the older and more conservative members of the church. The piece was as truly a theatrical representation as if it had been "Toodles" or "The Irish Schoolmaster;" and it is due to the pious discrimination of the critics to say that they recognized it. The church had been turned into a theatre. On the repetition of the exhibition the following week, it was given without costumes. The effect of seeing Pharaoh and Moses reduced to black coats was somewhat dispiriting both to players and audience. It had the tameness which the dramatic part of an oratorio always has when compared with an opera. The ideal and moral part of the play had been all the stronger for being more truthful as a representation. Dramatic fire, however, had been kindled in the bosom of the pastor's son. The exchange of the king's robes for a broadcloth suit could not quench it. He was thoroughly stage-struck, and to the horror of the church, and to the pain of his family and friends, soon after went upon the stage, and entered into the hardships and vicissitudes of an actor's life.

Perhaps the time may come when it will be deemed no more strange for a minister's son to become an actor, especially if he be a good one, than to be a painter, a public reader, or to enter any field of representative art. The stigma attached to this choice is largely the result of unjust prejudice and of Puritanic ideas concerning the gulf which should separate the Church from spectacular amusements. The associations of the actor, however, have not always been such as to command either respect or confidence. It is a reproach to the Church that it has not lent its influence toward the refinement and purification of this form of art.

To Asked-of-God, however, there was no temptation to go to the theatre, circus, or any other form of secular amusement. He found all the interest and satisfaction that he needed in the regular and constant engagements of the church. In revival seasons, when the religious sentiment was superheated, no time was left for anything else but the salvation of sinners. He threw himself into this work with great heartiness. The whole ward in the neighborhood of the church was divided into districts, which were thoroughly canvassed by tract distributors. Armed with bundles of tracts and with printed invitations to the church meetings, the young convert attacked several of the tenement-houses in the vicinity. It was at first somewhat embarrassing to knock at the door of a strange family and proffer a tract. The embarrassment was increased when some belligerent Romanist slammed the door in the visitor's face, threatened him with a broomstick, or, as happened on one occasion to a companion, threw a cat at the intruder. But did not the Master say, "Blessed are ye when men shall revile you and persecute you, and say all manner of evil against you falsely for my sake. Rejoice and be exceeding glad"? Such treatment was but evidence of the genuineness of the victim's Christianity.

Another work which interested Asked-of-God, and a work which he assumed entirely on his own account, was the distribution of tracts and other gospel appeals to the sailors. Every Sunday morning before breakfast, an hour or two was spent in this work, and an hour or two in the afternoon. The young missionary was provided with tracts in eight or ten different languages. English, French, German, Norwegian, Danish, Dutch, Italian, Spanish, Portuguese, were sometimes all used in the course of the Sunday, as the distributor moved along from dock to dock, and climbed from vessel to vessel, not without occasional risk of a ducking, and not always to the advantage of Sunday go-to-meeting clothes. The boy's mother, having remarked on one occasion that he brought home an unusual quantity of tar on his new suit, smiled affectionately at his earnestness when he answered, "Go into all the world and preach my gospel, but do not soil your clothes!" There was no sacrifice that the young convert in his ardor was not willing to make to save sinners from the fearful hell that awaited them, and to win them to the joy that comes from belief in Christ. For this cause the worst slums in the vilest portion of the city were visited with a companion, prayer-meetings were held, and earnest but wishy-washy exhortations were offered. Wishy-washy they seem now: they did not seem so then, when addressed to men who were standing on "slippery places, while fiery billows rolled beneath."

Still another field of work was found in the large establishment containing several hundred workmen, in which Asked-of-God was then serving in the humble capacity of errand boy. After his conversion, he considered himself as an errand boy for Christ. He deemed it a part of his daily duty to invite the workmen to the revival meetings, and to speak with them in regard to the condition of their souls. It was a source of satisfaction on going home on Saturday night to think that he had invited forty or fifty men that day to attend the services on the morrow. Who could tell but the Holy Spirit might send some shaft into their hearts? But the boy could not be wholly and absolutely merged in the young convert, and there is still left a lingering sense of the keen condemnation with which he went home on another Saturday night with the consciousness that he had wasted most of his leisure time in playing with a lively goat in the back yard of the office instead of inviting sinners to Christ.

These varied Christian activities, combined with a superfluity of prayer-meetings, so completely absorbed the youth's time that there was little left for either amusement or study, unless it was the study of the Bible, which was ardently pursued. A schedule of the ordinary and regular church services will account for a large portion of Asked-of-God's time, in addition to the fifty-nine hours a week which he spent in earning his daily bread: —

Sunday. From 6 to 8 A. M., Distributing tracts among the seamen. 8 to 9, Breakfast. 9 to 10.30, Sunday-school. 10.30 to 12, Church service. 12 to 1.30 P. M., Dinner. 1.30 to 3.30, Tract-distributing. 3.30 to 5, Prayer-meeting in the large auditorium of the church. 6 o'clock, Supper. 6.30 to 7.30, Prayer-meeting, attended by a few of the faithful to pray for a blessing on the evening service. 7.30 to 9, Preaching, usually followed by baptism.

Services on the other days of the week were confined to the evening, and were, —

Monday. Inquiry meeting.

Tuesday. Lecture by the pastor, usually an expository service of about an hour, preceded by singing and prayer.

Wednesday. Bible class.

Thursday. Young people's prayer-meeting.

Friday. Regular prayer-meeting of the church, which all were expected to attend.

In revival seasons, prayer-meeting was also held on Saturday evening. Sometimes these services gave way during revivals to preaching, which took place every night in the week. A boys' prayer-meeting, in which youths of from twelve to eighteen years of age assembled at each other's homes to pray for the salvation of their comrades, flourished for a short time; but as the solemnity of the meetings was followed by a reaction of excessive hilarity, the pastor had too much good sense to approve of it, and it was wisely abandoned.

To an apathetic Christian the list of Sunday services described may seem formidable. To Asked-of-God there was no day in the week to which he looked forward with so much delight as the recurrence of the Sabbath day, as it was inappropriately called. No amount of services could dampen the ardor of the young convert. There are no hours so precious as those which we spend in religious contemplation or in performing services for a "lost" or imperilled humanity, even though the peril may be wholly fictitious. And if, on some Sunday night, Asked-of-God went with a sense of weariness to his couch, there was the sweet consciousness of duty well done, and the blessed assurance that "they that be wise shall shine as the brightness of the firmament, and they that turn many to righteousness as the stars forever and ever."

IX.

THE PRAYER-MEETING.

IT must not be inferred from the previous chapter that Asked-of-God was without dissipation. His dissipations, however, were almost entirely of a religious character. He was intoxicated with religious emotion. While he confessed much joy in the hearing of the Word, the prayer-meeting was the chief source of exhilaration. The regular and most representative prayer and conference meeting was held on Friday evening, in what was known as the lecture-room, in the basement of the church. The room was devoid of all pictures or ornaments, and preserved a sober, Puritanic simplicity. The benches were uncushioned, the floor uncarpeted. Although there was no written law to this effect, yet it was the established custom for the male and female members to separate as soon as they entered the door, the women sitting on the right side of the main aisle facing the pulpit, and the men on the left. In revival times, the room was well filled; and the meeting went off with lively interest, without any of those long and dreadful pauses which indicated "leanness of soul" and vacuity of intellect. The pastor invariably led the Friday-night meeting. It was understood that he was simply to guide, direct, inspire, and on rare occasions to modify or restrain. The meeting belonged to the people.

The pastor was a little man, physically considered; but he always made an impression upon the stranger as he walked up the aisle with an air of confidence and self-assertion. He "magnified his office." He took his seat behind the plain wooden desk.

"Let us sing the 358th hymn."

What the 358th hymn was I do not exactly remember, but it may stand for any one of a dozen familiar hymns which were relied upon to set the meeting in motion. In times of religious declension, the favorite opening hymn was, —

"Come, Holy Spirit, heavenly dove,
With all thy quickening powers."

In revival times, more energetic and joyful hymns set the tone of the meeting. The hymn being sung, the pastor announced that Deacon C. would lead them in prayer, followed by Brother John Smith. The pastor believed in training the young converts, and he had a habit of hitching up a young colt with an old wheel-horse in the prayer-meeting exercises. The writer has not forgotten the terror that suddenly seized him when, a few weeks after his conversion, the pastor announced in prayer-meeting that Deacon B. would lead them in prayer, followed by Brother Asked-of-God. The pastor did not do this in cold blood: it was his kindly theory that an introductory prayer by Brother B. would give the young fledgling a chance to flap his little wings and prepare for a spiritual flight on his own account. Had he asked the young convert to pray first, the task he assigned him would have been far easier, as it is always easier to plunge at once into the stream than to stand shivering on the bank. It was not reassuring to the convert to be asked to follow such a practised and self-reliant devotee as Deacon B. He pictured in his mind the contrast between the regular, measured cadence of the deacon's solemn supplications and his own broken, stammering, incoherent utterances. The period occupied by Deacon B.'s prayer was one of actual torture to the youth who was to follow. Instead of putting him in a state of spiritual fervor, it bathed him in a cold sweat. He was in no condition to formulate expressions and arrange thoughts during the deacon's prayer. His mind seemed suddenly emptied of everything that it had previously contained. The fire of emotion was extinguished. Feeling very much like a young culprit, he sat in the pew and waited tremblingly for the deacon to finish, praying inwardly that the consummation of his petition might be postponed as long as possible. The deacon seldom soared very high in his prayers; but he circled round and round like a bird with heavy wing, and one could not always tell when and where he would alight. Sometimes it would seem as if he had told the Lord everything that he knew, and asked him for everything that was desirable, and that the prayer must come to an end at the next period; but Asked-of-God would take a new breath when he found that the deacon, like a practised seaman, meant to make another tack before he lowered sail and dropped anchor.

When, finally, the young convert found that his fate could no longer be postponed, he yielded to the necessity. The deacon had already exhausted the whole subject; and there was nothing left for him but to utter a few platitudes of supplication in the conventional prayer-meeting dialect.

After the prayer-meeting had once been set in motion, it was expected to move of its own accord and with increased velocity. In revival times, when there was a stiff breeze of religious interest, the sails were well filled, and the meeting seemed to scud along as if impelled by that mighty wind "which bloweth where it listeth." At other times the meeting lay to like a ship becalmed. All that the pastor could do at the rudder or the deacons at the oars did not avail to send it forward. There were no fish caught in such a lull. Converts could not be taken, like cod, with the vessel at anchor; they must be drawn in, like blue-fish, with the vessel skimming along under a rattling breeze.

While Scripture reading formed a part of the opening exercises, the means mainly relied upon to keep the meeting in motion were the force of song and exhortation. The first few hymns were formally announced by the pastor. After that, any one in the congregation could interpolate a hymn whenever the spirit moved. The pastor had a powerful voice; his singing was noted more for volume of tone than for sweetness of expression. He could bring in the appropriate hymn, however, with great effect. He would occasionally edify the congregation by singing as a solo some hymn which he had recently acquired. Of course there was no objection to any one joining in; but as nobody else knew it, the pastor generally had it his own way. The Moody and Sankey hymns had not yet invaded the public ear. There were other revival melodies, however, which formed a contrast to the stately solemnity and dull monotony of some of the older tunes. A favorite hymn with the pastor was one beginning, —

> "How lost was my condition
> Till Jesus made me whole!
> There is but one Physician
> Can cure the sin-sick soul."

Another represented a colloquy between a passenger on the gospel ship and one who asked him concerning the conditions and destination of the voyage. Canaan was indicated as the destination, and wine, milk, and honey as the fare of the fortunate resident of that clime. The hymn was interspersed with "hallelujahs."

A favorite hymn of the young convert was, —

> "O happy day that fixed my choice
> On thee, my Saviour and my God,"

sung to one of Mr. Bradbury's tunes. Another favorite was, —

> "I'm happy, I'm happy, I'm on my way to glory;
> I'm happy, I'm happy, I'm on my journey home."

There were others appealing to sinners, such as —

> "Will you go, will you go?"

Sunday-school hymnals had just been invigorated and refreshed by a new set of hymns, such as "Sweet Hour of Prayer," "Homeward Bound," "The Shining Shore," and many others; and these soon found their way into the prayer-meeting. But the old stand-bys, such as "There is a fountain filled with blood," "Alas! and did my Saviour bleed?" "Broad is the road that leads to death," and many others of Watts's and Doddridge's hymns, were not neglected.

Nearly all the hymns were undenominational. The writer recalls, however, the words and tune of a solo which was sung on one occasion by a woman in the audience, and which he never heard repeated:—

> "Once I heard a Baptist preach,
> His words they to my heart did reach:
> He said I must be born again,
> If ever heaven I would obtain."

In revival seasons, the exhortations were short and fervid. There were brief statements of experience from the young converts. A large part of the time was taken up with this testimony. Sometimes all that a convert would say was, "I love Jesus," and then sit down again. Though members were called upon to pray, they were never called upon to speak. There was a general expectation, however, that all would take part when the spirit moved. To sensitive and retiring natures, it was regarded as a great cross to speak in meeting. How often did Asked-of-God go home from the prayer-meeting with a sense of condemnation that he had let some opportunity slip of bearing testimony for Jesus! A sure way of enjoying the meeting was to take part yourself.

Once a month, however, was held what is known as covenant meeting, on the Friday night before the communion service. At this meeting it was the custom for the deacons to relate their religious experience for the past month. Then, beginning on the front row of seats, each of the members in order gave in his or her testimony. This is what may be called the Baptist confessional. While some had a cheerful word of gratitude or faith to utter, most of the addresses were penitential confessions of leanness of spirit and coldness of heart; and such a meeting seldom passed by without the hymn being sung, —

> "Oh for a closer walk with God,
> A calm and heavenly frame."

On Thursday evening a young people's prayer-meeting was held. Here the voice of the young doves found it much easier to coo. This meeting formed an excellent gymnasium in which the youthful portion of the congregation could exercise their spiritual gifts; and one of the first responsibilities which Asked-of-God incurred at the age of fourteen was the conduct of this meeting.

As the writer looks back upon these meetings, he recalls the warmth of religious emotion, the grateful sense of Christian fellowship, and the constant assurance of the favor of God purchased through the death of Christ, which they developed. In a time of religious interest, these prayer and conference meetings were a source of continual satisfaction. Looking at them now, however, from a wider experience and with a more impartial and by no means an unsympathetic judgment, several serious limitations must be noticed.

1. *They abounded in earnestness, but not in devotion.* This may seem an extraordinary statement; but, so far as the writer's observation is concerned, it is correct. There was an abundance of fervor, but little of the calm, trustful spirit of a peaceful and profound devotion. There was the rush and the roar of the brook, but not the depth and placidity of the lake. The type of earnestness in religious exercise found its most extreme expression in the old Methodist prayer-meeting, where the devotee shouted as if God were deaf, and a chorus of explosive amens urged him to still greater feats of lung power. But a strong degree of earnestness may exist with a comparatively weak degree of reverence. Under the name of piety and devotion there was much fervid and ill-timed extravagance. The Baptist prayer-meetings were not of the shouting kind, but they were conducted generally under a false idea of the nature of prayer. Notwithstanding the warning of Jesus to the contrary, it seemed to be assumed in prayer-meeting that men were "to be heard for their much speaking." God was a being to be supplicated. The parable of the unjust judge was often used to illustrate the importunity necessary to influence God's will. It was often said, "Prayer moves the arm that moves the universe." There was seldom a prayer offered of pure adoration, of deep meditative, spiritual

communion. They were rather arguments founded on Scripture promises, exhortations to God, mournful confessions of sin, and earnest invocations of his mercy for lost souls. That there were personal exceptions to this need hardly be said; but I am speaking now of the average prayer-meeting and its essential characteristics.

2. *They were generally stereotyped and mechanical.* The use of any form of liturgy except the hymn-book would have been stoutly resisted. It was assumed that it was not best to take any thought concerning what one should say, especially in his prayers: the Spirit would give utterance as was needed. Notwithstanding, few of the brethren had versatility enough to avoid painful and monotonous repetitions. Deacon F.'s prayer, for instance, was always exactly the same. It was written on his brain — and I am sure it was written on his heart — as certainly as if it had been written or printed in a book. When he dropped on his knees, the writer, after hearing him a few times, did not need to *follow* his prayer, but invariably kept a sentence or two ahead. Indeed, that prayer was so deeply impressed upon my memory that it would not be difficult for me to recite half of it now.

Occasionally the monotony of the prayer-meeting was broken by an earnest exhortation from old Aunt Rachel, a venerable colored woman, who spoke with a rugged, picturesque eloquence and an originality of expression which produced amusement, if not conviction.

3. *Another defect of these meetings was that they had no immediate practical relation to life.* I do not mean that they

did not develop religious feeling, that they did not encourage a high moral tone. I mean that the *emphasis* of these meetings was laid on a preparation for the next world rather than upon a preparation for this one. Hence the practical problems of daily life were never considered. Schemes of education, charity, reform, or any type of active benevolence, were never broached there. The explanation of this was in the theology on which the prayer-meeting was built. When it was assumed that the greater part of the human race is rushing down the broad road to endless misery, what more important work could the church undertake than the salvation of as many as God had decreed to be saved by the prayers and efforts of his people? What was any work to save the poor from the distresses of poverty, to raise the standard of culture, or to beautify the place of this human life below, compared with the imperative duty of snatching sinners as brands from the eternal burning? What were a few years in comfort here compared with an endless future beyond? Accepting this theology, the church was perfectly consistent, and showed a genuine but mistaken spirit of benevolence in neglecting the minor interests of men in this world for the sake of their eternal interests beyond.

X.

GETTING THEOLOGY.

ASKED-OF-GOD had "got religion." The next step in his experience was to get theology. These two elements were not entirely distinct. It was necessary to have a tincture of theology with one's religion, in order to enter the church at all. But it was only the milk of theology, not the strong meat, that was given to the babes. A belief in the ruin wrought by Adam's sin, a consciousness that one had partaken of his guilt and repeated his disobedience, a belief in the threatened penalty of everlasting punishment and in redemption through Christ as an atoning Saviour, — these theological rudiments were supposed to be the A B C's of a convert's knowledge. As already said, no creed or catechism was used. The church covenant was simply a pledge of mutual love and watch-care. Few of the converts by their own volition went beyond the theological primer. In the Bible-class knotty questions often arose; but they mainly related to Scripture exegesis.

Asked-of-God found, however, that, apart from the emotional glow which he had felt in his conversion, there was an intellectual side to religion, which opened up a wide and inviting field of speculation. He entered it with all the avidity with which an enthusiastic astronomer goes to his telescope or a studious biologist to his microscope. Theology is but another term for a philosophy of the universe. Here was human life on one side, with its facts and its mysteries, one as perplexing as the other. Here was eternity on the other side, with its vast depths of being, its unsolved enigmas, its awful possibilities. As there was a science of man, was there not also a science of God? Hitherto the Bible had been to him a good book, full of moral and religious precepts, many of which he had learned at his mother's knee. He now viewed it in a new light. It became a theological text-book. It contained a profound revelation from God, and the young convert sought to comprehend its intellectual height and depth.

The regular Baptist churches of America have been uniformly Calvinistic. We believe there is as yet but one Free Will Baptist Church in New York. ' It was not uncommon, however, and it is becoming still more frequent, to find many Arminians in heart in individual Baptist churches. Both of these schools were represented in this Baptist meeting-house. The female members took little or no interest in theology as a science. The majority of the male members were of the working class, who looked at the practical side of religion as they looked at the practical side of life, and paid little attention to subtilties of philosophy. But the pastor had enough theology for the whole congregation, and dealt it out in liberal instalments. He was not, however, the chief theologian of the church. He had undertaken the tasks of life at an early age, and after a varied course of experience had entered the ministry without the preparation of a full theological course. He found, after settlement in New York, an unprofessional theological tutor in the person of a venerable and eccentric admirer of his preaching. This member, Brother C., was a man of much intellectual and personal force and of pronounced individuality. Though his scholarship was not profound, it was broad and varied, especially in the department of theology. He was an intense hyper-Calvinist. He knew every beam and pillar, every stone in the foundation of the Calvinistic system. In his mind, it was as grand and as perfect as if God had dictated its dimensions and its structure, as he was said to have built the Jewish temple, by his word. Brother C. knew the New Testament almost by heart. Not consecutively, however. With consummate art he had arranged all its passages into a beautiful mosaic, the subject of which, brought out in vivid colors, was the plan of salvation.

It would be hard to find a more typical representative of the uncompromising Calvinist of olden times than Brother C. He was not only a Calvinist by education, but one by nature. He was tall and erect in person. The back part of his head was very high, indicating phrenologically a large stock of firmness and self-esteem. His moral strength and dignity of character were impressive. He was earnest, vehement, and peculiarly eccentric in manner. His features were prominent, his head almost entirely bald, presumably from the effect of too much fire within. He had a retentive memory, a ready command of language, and was acknowledged to be the most influential theological leader in the church. He never arose in prayer-meeting unless he had something to say. His expositions of Scripture were considered to be quite as authoritative as those of the pulpit. Indeed, it was soon recognized by such of the members as applied themselves to theological study that the pastor himself was but a disciple of Brother C. with the rest. Being more than twice as old as the pastor, and far more widely read in theology, he became his constant counsellor and guide. He was a self-constituted censor in the pew. Having pre-empted a regular seat in the prayer-meeting at one side of the pulpit, no one thought of taking it any more than of taking the pastor's chair in the pulpit. In the church he invariably sat at the end of his pew, with his head leaning on his hand, supported by his elbow on the back of the seat. His eyes were closed. He seldom or never looked at the preacher. There was no suspicion of slumber, however, in his case; for his head was in almost constant motion, assenting in affirmative nods, often accompanied by corroborative groans, to the pastor's exposition of his favorite themes of God's sovereignty and redemption. When a strange preacher came, however, who was suspected of being less rigidly Calvinistic, his ear was more than usually alert; and when any passage occurred in the sermon which contradicted his favorite system, he would shake his head in decisive denial. Anybody who sat near Brother C. could always tell, therefore, whether he liked the sermon.

His head was an oscillating theological gauge. The young convert often consulted the indicator at doubtful points in the progress of the sermon. Brother C. did not publicly dissent at any time from the preaching of the pastor, who was too thoroughly imbued with his master's teaching. But on one occasion the pastor, having made some unguarded theological statement which threatened the symmetry of the theological system, corrected himself the following week, and affirmed a modified form of the doctrine. Every one knew who had administered the correction.

Asked-of-God was early singled out as one whom God might be pleased to call to the ministry. Sooner or later he believed that he had passed through this experience. The call, as it came to him, was but a ratification of early aspirations. Two distinct and positive peaks of ambition loomed up in his childish desires: one was an ambition to be a stage-driver; the other the ambition to be a minister. These somewhat conflicting desires struggled for pre-eminence. The boy did not find it difficult to combine them. One Sunday, for instance, on which he and his little sister were allowed to stay at home from church on account of the rain, the mother was surprised, on her return, to find two chairs harnessed up to an imaginary coach, the boy acting as driver and the little sister as passenger. The explanation of this secular exercise of the imagination on the Sabbath day was that the children had been "playing church," but on account of the wet state of the weather had deemed it best to drive the congregation to and from the house of worship. Church-playing was a familiar pastime, and the writer remembers an occasion when it was conducted with such seriousness that the boy and girl made a resolve in consequence to "be good" the rest of the week. The reality of religion and its relation to practical life were felt at that early day. It may seem paradoxical that a boy who could take refuge under a bed in order to escape from the affliction of a visit from the minister should aspire to be a minister himself; but such was the case, and I conclude that his aversion to the members of the profession was more particular than general.

The call that now came to him after his conversion was an utterance of the still small voice bringing him what seemed a commission to preach the gospel to a lost world. With what palpitating self-distrust and misgiving it came! Yet it came, too, with a "woe unto me if I preach not." The desire, confessed to a few, was tenderly encouraged; and Asked-of-God soon began to shape his studies with reference to this purpose in life. He was taken in hand by the pastor and Brother C., and was soon saturated with Calvinistic literature. It became his meat and his drink. He studied its angles and proportions, its theorems and corollaries, with as much delight as a mathematician would study the highest problems of his science. It was the custom for the minister to preach Sunday morning to "the saints" and Sunday night to "the sinners." The doctrine of election was his hobby, and he rode it so often in the pulpit as to weary some of his hearers. To Asked-of-

God, however, the doctrine was an unfailing source of delight, more so, it must be admitted, than the complementary doctrine of reprobation, which was preached with merciless power. The pastor not only believed that God had called men before the foundation of the world by the election of grace, but he also believed that God had deliberately reprobated others to eternal damnation. It was truly a terrible doctrine; and the pastor never preached it in cold blood, but as if it were a funeral sermon of lost souls. With all its horrors, it belonged in the Calvinistic system. Calvinism is emasculated without it.

The Arminian sentiment of the church was not organized and not very strong intellectually. Its acknowledged representative was Deacon A., a man as different from Brother C. as were the systems which they supported. Deacon A. was a simple ship-carpenter, without culture, humble in spirit, devout, and far more emotional than intellectual in his cast of mind. He knew, however, just where to find the Arminian passages in the Bible. While Brother C. insisted that no one could come unto Jesus except the Father drew him, Deacon A. replied with a "Ho! every one that thirsteth," or "Come unto me, all ye that labor and are heavy-laden." Brother C. believed that "God shall send them strong delusion, that they should believe a lie: that they all might be damned who believed not the truth, but had pleasure in unrighteousness." Deacon A. replied, "As I live, saith the Lord, I have no pleasure in the death of the wicked, but that the wicked turn from his way and live." The reason why men did not come unto God was because they did not *will* to do so. "Ye will not come unto me, that ye might have life." Brother C. contended that none could be converted unless the Holy Spirit first moved their hearts. Deacon A. simply urged them to come and be saved. "I do not believe," Deacon A. once said to the young convert, "that God ties men down, and then asks them to come unto him." In prayer-meeting, the two leaders were entirely different. Brother C. always rose to his full height when he addressed God in prayer; Deacon A. with characteristic humility fell upon his knees. Brother C. extolled the majesty of God; Deacon A. seemed to feel the littleness of man. Brother C. was always self-possessed and never lost his mental poise; Deacon A. poured out his soul in prayer with a torrent of emotion. Their Scriptural expositions were often contradictory. Brother C. watched over the interests of his pupils with a lynx-eyed vigilance. He took care that Deacon A.'s loose expositions of Scripture should not pervert them. On one occasion, at a prayer-meeting, after Deacon A. had been enlarging upon the perfect liberty of the sinner to come unto God, Brother C., with dignified self-control, ventured no public reply. As they were leaving the room, however, at the close of the meeting, he passed by Asked-of-God at the door, and whispered into his ear with great positiveness, "I do not believe *one word that man has said.*" Asked-of-God knew that he did not. He found it difficult at first to reconcile this contradictory theology. His mind could not obey the scientific law that when a body is acted upon by two forces moving in opposite directions, it should pass in a straight line between them. The pressure, however, was not equal. It was too strong in one direction, and Asked-of-God soon became as rabid a Calvinist as the pastor or his instructor. He had got theology. Perhaps he had got too much of it.

XI.

AN INSIDE VIEW OF CALVINISM.

"I LOVE," said John Cotton, "to sweeten my mouth with a piece of John Calvin before I go to sleep." To a modern liberal theologian, Calvinistic doctrine, pure and simple, does not seem to furnish a very good narcotic. To unsympathetic minds, it is a wonder that any tongue should find sweet morsels in it. It seems a compound of the roots of all bitterness without even a dressing of sugar to make it palatable. A lady once remarked to the writer, after hearing a candid exposition of Calvinism as a moral force, that she did not see how any one could possibly have endured that system; it seemed to her utterly dark and joyless. Much naturally depends upon the angle from which we view it. It is with this as with other outgrown forms of thought: to estimate its power, we must view it from the inside, from the standpoint of the believer. We need not assume that this standpoint is a true one. It furnishes, nevertheless, the base line from which we may survey the believer's religious position. When Calvin lived, an entirely different view of the earth and its relation to the universe was taken from that which now prevails. The difference between the Ptolemaic and the Copernican system is immense. It is the difference between truth and falsehood. Nevertheless, though the believer in the Ptolemaic system was radically wrong in his assumptions, this did not prevent him from enjoying the grandeur of the starlit heavens or the warmth and brilliancy of the sun whose motion he had misconceived. In order to sympathize with the Hindu, the Roman, and the Greek, when we examine their religions, we must put ourselves in their places. In a similar manner, we must provisionally admit the premises of Calvinism, to form any idea of its power upon the heart, mind, and life of one who accepted it.

The fundamental premises of that system may here be briefly restated. By his disobedience in the garden, Adam had brought ruin upon himself and the whole human family. This disobedience had been foreseen by God. He had, however, taken no steps to prevent it. Man by his rebellion had incurred the penalty of eternal and unspeakable misery. Of this penalty God was in no wise bound to relieve him. In the councils of eternity, his Son freely offered to come to earth, robe himself in human flesh, and give himself as a ransom for those whom God, according to the pleasure of his own will, should choose to be saved from eternal woe. The number thus chosen was conceived to be but a small proportion of the human race. It was assumed that those thus elected would be called, sanctified, and saved. Nothing whatever could prevent this consummation, which was indescribably glorious on the one hand, as the damnation of the sinner was indescribably horrible on the other. Calvinistic divines always confessed a sense of limit in two directions. They could never paint heaven so grand or hell so black as they believed them to be.

This brief outline of Calvinism was the framework in which the religious conceptions of Asked-of-God were woven. To the Calvinist, it was a framework of gold; to those who were doomed by it, it was as black as ebony.

Notice for a moment what elements of comfort there were for one who not only believed in the truth of the system, but also felt that it had been applied to his own redemption.

1. *A sense of the sovereignty of God.* God was uniformly pictured in his governmental rather than in his parental relationship. It was assumed that he had power to do whatever he pleased to do. While it was taken for granted that he could not do wrong, the kind of justice that he exercised was one which fell far below our best human standards. Whatever God willed, was assumed to be just. Softer-hearted Calvinists, and those of fine moral discrimination often sought to apologize for the acts of God; but to the thorough-going Calvinist, apology was superfluous. God's will itself fixed the standard of justice. He was a king who could not be tried for his acts by any of his subjects. There was a grim grandeur about this conception of God. He moved through the universe in stately and ineffable majesty. He wrought everything after the stern pleasure of his own will. Honor and glory enveloped his throne. His sceptre was the

law of the world. If this was awful and fear-inspiring to those who opposed his commands, it meant confidence, safety, victory for those who were the subjects of his favor. Nothing was more certain than that God would save his own elect. The Calvinist's faith never wavered here. It did sometimes waver in regard to the assurance of his own election. When this was once a fixed conviction, his destiny was as sure as that of God himself.

2. *The election of grace.* Imagine yourself to have been personally thought of by the Triune Council before the foundation of the world. Suppose that, then and there, your name was written in the Book of Life as a chosen vessel, as one to be redeemed by the sacrifice of Christ. This choice was made and this salvation conferred by no merit of yours, but simply because the Triune God preferred you to millions who, so far as their life in this world is concerned, were to be infinitely better. Who that was able to persuade himself of the truth of his own election could fail to entertain an unusual degree of personal happiness in regard to his own future welfare? It was only when the elected saint thought of the defeated candidates that the noon of his joy became clouded with pity.

The doctrine of election seems at first to be one only suited to the selfish and egotistic mind. Who but an egotist, we may ask, could feel profoundly convinced that God had chosen him in the councils of eternity, to the utter exclusion of a vast multitude of his fellow-beings? Yet, as a fact, Calvinism was accepted and believed by a large number of humble people. One of the graces which it constantly enforced was the grace of humility. Redemption was a system of marvels, and it was a constant wonder to the humble-minded believer, as well it might be, that God had chosen him instead of choosing somebody else.

Another consideration that provoked humility was that personal merit had nothing to do with this choice. The man who led a truly moral and noble life was just as likely to be lost as one who did not. The thief on the cross who repented at the last moment was one of the elect; the young man who had kept the law from his youth may have been reprobated to eternal damnation.

3. *The witness of the Spirit.* It was important, it will be seen, to fix the assurance of personal salvation. This was conveyed by the supposed witness of the Spirit. "The Spirit witnesseth with our spirit that we are the sons of God." If we look at the biographies of many Calvinists, we shall see that this spiritual assurance was by no means constant. There were times of great depression, when doubts of their calling and election came over them. Favor with God did not depend merely upon resolving to do your duty to-day and to-morrow: the important question was whether, at a certain spiritual crisis in the previous history of the individual, his conversion was genuine, and whether the Spirit continued to witness to its truth. Floods of tears, millions of groans, an incalculable number of sleepless nights and weary, sombre days, have been passed in settling this question.

Self-deception was supposed to be common. The individual must carefully distinguish between his own desire to be saved, and the witness of the Spirit that he really had been saved. Yet no sufficient tests were furnished to make this distinction certain. Thus, if the Calvinist sometimes passed into a state of super-exaltation, an almost wild delirium of joy in the unbounded confidence of his salvation, he often had to pay for this by seasons of deep depression. When we think of the fears which Calvinism sought to excite in the unconverted, and of the future misery which it promised to the unrepentant sinner, we discover a poetic justice in the waves of doubt and despondency which sometimes swept over those who were supposed to enjoy its richest consolations.

4. *Gratitude for salvation.* This was one of the greatest motive forces in Calvinism. "We love him because he first loved us." The sinner had been condemned to the dark and ceaseless torments of hell. He had hung over the deep abyss, powerless to save himself. God, in the exercise of his marvellous mercy, had interposed, and plucked him as a brand from the burning. Why should he not be grateful to God for his pardoning grace, and to Christ, through whose sacrificial death his redemption had been wrought? Would not the condemned criminal feel a thrill of gratitude toward him who had sent his pardon as well as to the one who had suffered in his stead? This sense of obligation was a constant incentive to the convert to do all that he could to promote the glory of a

vainglorious God, and to show his love to the Christ whose blood had saved him.

These elements in Calvinism — the sovereignty of God, the election of grace, the witness of the Spirit, the perseverance of the saints, the assured promise of eternal bliss, and the sense of gratitude and obligation which these awakened — were forms and forces of belief which made Calvinism a tower of strength to those who stood within it. But the tower cast a long and deep shadow for those who were on the outside.

XII.

TRANSITIONS.

THE doctrine of the perseverance of the saints is a favorite theory of Calvinistic Baptists. It is a doctrine which is put to severe tests. Experience and observation show that there are large numbers of converts who, to all outward appearance, are sadly lacking in the virtue of perseverance. The presumption in such cases is either that they were never truly converted, or that they will eventually return to their first love. It was not long before there was a reaction in the old meeting-house. The excitement passed away, the attendance dropped off with the coming of warm weather. The parable of the sower received a new illustration. Some had received the word in stony ground. It had sprung up joyfully at first, but withered under the scorching heat of temptation. The cares of this world and the deceitfulness of riches — and quite as frequently the obstructions of poverty — checked the growth of others. The preaching was once more directed against "the backslider in heart."

Few of the converts who entered the church with confident gladness realized how short would be their connection with it. One of the younger members, as already noticed, was expelled for repeatedly attending the theatre. Another young man suddenly left for Canada, under conditions of surprise and distress to his friends. A bright and promising young man, who had begun to study for the ministry, was expelled from the church after a trial on charges affecting his good character, and subsequently found a drunkard's grave. South America furnished an asylum for another, who figured as an escaped forger. The falls from grace, however, were not generally moral falls; they were mainly lapses into worldliness and religious indifference. It would be unsafe to say what proportion of the converts proved faithful to their covenant vows. Probably not more than a fourth of them.

Two other candidates were baptized on the same night with Asked-of-God. Who of them thought for a moment on that joyful evening that the time would come when all three would be dropped or expelled from the Church they were about to join? It is a melancholy task to record the defeat of earnest aims and purposes. Three years from the night of his baptism, the dark-haired sailor, the first of the three to enter the baptismal water, was formally expelled from the church for intoxication. There is an entry in the journal of Asked-of-God recording this solemn fact, with an additional lament that the woman who formed the third in the trio was no longer seen at prayer-meeting or at church, — that her trust in Christ had evidently departed. "But if they are true believers," was the comment, "or ever were truly converted, He will bring them back to his fold again."

Asked-of-God did not realize, as he wrote this, that he himself would eventually be an outcast from the same fellowship, though for entirely different reasons. In previous chapters we have described how he entered the old Baptist meeting-house. In those that remain, it will be appropriate, and we hope not wholly unprofitable, to describe how he left it. In the case of the sailor, a few glasses of liquor were the occasion. With Asked-of-God, it was the intoxication of a new faith. It took ten long years to get it fully into his blood. To many members of the old church, we fear that the intemperance of the sailor and the spiritual indifference of the woman, which alienated her from the church, were less heinous than the "pestilential heresy" with which he became inoculated. Let it not be thought that he escaped the influence of the spiritual declension which came over the church. Many pages of paper, and much ink, and still more valuable time were wasted in recording the groaning self-accusations of a morbid, introverted self-consciousness. The diary served as a hair-shirt, as penitential peas in the boots. The difficulty was largely in the false standard which was set for the Christian life. Feeling rather than principle was made the test of experience. The absence of the first ecstatic joy of conversion was counted as a sad lapse into a lower spiritual state. The convert found that the battle of life was to be fought, not while soaring in the air on the eagle wings of his new hope, but while walking and working on the solid earth. There was a man of sin within, and there were many times when Paul's cry went up, "O wretched man that I am, who shall deliver me from the body of this sin and death?" It was not spiritual wretchedness, however, which banished the writer from the old church, but a new phase of intellectual and spiritual development.

Transitions of thought are often induced simply by transitions in space. When the environment changes, the material for our thought also changes. The mind gets a new point of view, it sees things from different angles; it has a new sense of proportion, and inevitably draws new comparisons, all of which lead to new conclusions. It would be false to assume that an intellectual or religious life is wholly at the mercy of its surroundings. It would be equally false to assume that it is not powerfully affected by them. It has been said, "When a man begins to eat Graham crackers, look out for his Orthodoxy." There is a presumption that when one accepts a new idea in one direction it opens his mind to the entrance of others. Graham crackers or not, the complexion of the mind is certainly affected by its mental diet. It may be interesting for students of heresy to know the forces which deflect men from Orthodoxy. In the case of Asked-of-God, it is as easy to find the switch-point of circumstance which gave his life a new direction as it is to measure the deviation it created.

When old Mother Costigan, on one bright autumn day, wrapped up another bundle of polyglot tracts in a newspaper, for distribution among the sailors, she was entirely innocent that it contained an advertisement which, though little heeded in itself, was influential in suggestion, and was to lead to important results in the life of this tract-distributor.

The advertisement ran thus: —

SHORT-HAND learned in fifteen minutes. After that, all that is necessary is practice. Send for charts to John Humbug, etc.

This was not the name given in the advertisement, and the address is forgotten. Asked-of-God never sent for the chart or placed any confidence in the lying statement it contained; but the question arose, Why not learn this valuable art? Our pastor preaches his eloquent sermons without notes. How fine it would be to take them down in short-hand and preserve them for humanity! Friends were consulted, the pastor highly favored the project, and offered, when the boy had scarcely mastered the alphabet, to open the study behind the pulpit, and furnish him a table every Sunday for the practice of the art. Brother C., the pastor's monitor, also encouraged it, and recalled the time when he had dabbled in stenography himself. A more cautious business friend consulted a New York reporter, and returned the discouraging reply that it would take months of hard application to learn the art; that not one in a hundred who began it became a verbatim reporter. His advice was, "Do not attempt it;" and Asked-of-God immediately decided that he would!

Who could have supposed that any heresy lurked in those hooks and curves and angles? It would not be just to invest the art with suspicions of this kind. The short-hand writer simply accustoms himself to take down with accuracy the opinions of other people. It was not, therefore, this book of pot-hooks which was responsible for the new direction of thought. It was rather the sphere of ideas to which they were applied. These stenographic characters were simply the curious keys that opened for the young scribe the doorway into a new realm of thought and occupation. Some other key might have answered as well if it had happened to fit the lock.

Dickens, in his "David Copperfield," has inimitably described the experience of the average stenographic student. Traddles never could make it go. Copperfield succeeded only after untiring labor. It is a study which requires an agile mind, deft fingers, and unremitting application. Asked-of-God often thought of the printed lie on the tract wrapper, — "Short-hand learned in fifteen minutes." But was there not added the reservation, "*All* that is necessary afterward is *practice*"? Finally, the mountain was tunnelled sufficiently far to get gleams of daylight. There was some hope of emerging at the other side. The student had pierced it with his lead-pencil, and used up a good many quires of paper in the process.

Studying the art at first simply to advance the kingdom of God by taking down the sermons of the minister, it then presented itself as a means of livelihood and as a stepping-stone to higher things. When, by dint of some labor, he had acquired a moderate degree of speed, he took up, one morning, a New York daily. An advertisement for a short-hand writer attracted his attention. He sent an application to Box 730, New York Post Office. How did his eyes happen to strike just that advertisement, which proved to be packed so full of consequence? He has often since pondered this question. Opportunities which we have seized, and which prove fruitful to us sometimes seem to have miraculous elements in them, just as the extraordinary draught of fishes seemed miraculous to the disciples. Yet all that was necessary was to cast the net on the right side of the ship.

After waiting day after day in vain for some notice of his application, and forgetting almost that he had made one, the incipient stenographer was attracted, one morning, by the ringing of the door-bell. The letter which the postman brought invited him, if not already engaged, to call at No. 308 Broadway. The call was made, a proposition followed, and finally an engagement was effected. For nine years, beginning at the tender age of nine, Asked-of-God had earned his bread, and a thin coating of butter, with one firm; and he might have been there still, if nothing had diverted the course of his life. One of the most difficult steps he has ever had to take was this, occurring at the age of eighteen, when he forced himself to break away from a clerkship in a great manufacturing establishment, under the shelter of kind kinsmen and with an assured prospect of a permanent position, to enter upon a new and untried field of life. Once taken, the resolution was adhered to with unwavering determination.

The place to which he went might have been called Golgotha, for it was literally a place of skulls. Who that has walked up Broadway has not seen them in the window-case, accompanied with plaster busts, carefully mapped out on the surface to show the topography within? It was not only a place of skulls, but a place of brains and kind hearts. Without discussing here the merits of phrenology as a system of mental science, which Horace Mann so highly commended, Asked-of-God simply wishes to record his gratitude to the New York firm which has been for so many years its champion in this country. A large number of capable stenographers have found here, under Dr. Nelson Sizer's patient and considerate tuition, an early school for practice and progress in the art; and no one ever went there without feeling sensible of the high moral tone of this house and its interest in social and philanthropic reforms. Many a young man has confessed with gratitude the intellectual and moral awakening which he there experienced. No pressure was ever brought to bear to change the religious convictions of the employés. The members of the firm were connected with evangelical churches. They are not responsible, therefore, for the heresy which overtook one of their young reporters. They are only responsible for encouraging him to think for himself. This is always a dangerous practice for one who wishes to remain within conventional boundaries. The only safe way to secure fixedness in religious belief, and conservatism in everything else, is to see that men and women think precisely as did their ancestors.

Asked-of-God cannot fail to have a high respect for the mission of the press, when he recalls the fact that two little advertisements, one of them casually discovered on the wrapper of a bundle of tracts, and the other detected in the crowded columns of a New York daily, were instrumental in changing the whole course of his life. For nothing in the world would he exchange the treasures of thought, friendship, affection, and religious faith to which they introduced him.

XIII.

A MILD CASE OF HERESY.

CAN the Ethiopian help changing his skin, or the leopard his spots? Not unless they drop into a state of hibernation, or take something to check the metamorphosis of tissue. The leopard may lick his spots with an air of confident self-acquaintance. The Ethiopian may persuade himself, as he looks into the glass, that he is surveying the same swarthy self that he saw there ten years ago. The leopard and the Ethiopian are mistaken. They have been dying every day, and coming to life again. They have been breaking down tissue and building it up. The leopard has had various new overcoats as his wardrobe has needed them. The negro has had from time to time a new skin, and indeed a new set of bones, like an umbrella which has been so often framed and so often covered that there is nothing but the constancy of its color to preserve its questionable identity.

Certain it is that the mind has an experience analogous to that of the body. Its development is through a twofold process of growth, — a process of breaking down and of building up. There is metamorphosis of thought as well as metamorphosis of tissue. If the breaking down goes on faster than the building up, there is emaciation and mental disorganization; if the building up goes on in a normal way, and faster than the elimination of mind tissue, there is growth, though there are diseases which result from a too rapid multiplication of cells.

This process cannot be unduly forced: the soul, like the body, must have time to germinate and grow after the law of its being. All growth is mysterious. But nothing is more mysterious than the evolution of a human mind. The conscious subject seems to himself but the spectator of his own development, and is often ignorant of how much he has done to help or to retard it.

When Asked-of-God joined the church, his mental attitude was that of unquestioning acceptance. If a necessary doctrine seemed weak, he set about to strengthen it. He opened his Bible, not so much to see if these things were so, but to *make* them so.

He was determined, for instance, that Paul should teach the doctrine of election; and Paul helped him a good deal in his determination. The Bible was made a hunting-ground for texts in support of preconceived theories. There is no book more malleable than the Bible under such treatment. One can prove, at least to his own satisfaction, almost anything he sets out to prove from its pages, — Calvinism or Arminianism, Trinitarianism or Unitarianism, a limited atonement or a universal one; the salvation of all or the salvation of a few; that the first day of the week should be kept sacred or that the seventh day is the true Sabbath; that it is not proper to marry a deceased wife's sister, or that it is lawful and commendable;

that slavery and polygamy are permitted and encouraged, or that they are condemned and forbidden; that the soul is immortal and that it is not immortal. All of these contrary propositions have been ingeniously deduced and vehemently maintained from a book supposed by those who held them to be infallible. They have agreed that it could not err, and have determined that it *should* not err; and the easiest way to protect its infallibility has been to make it teach just what it has seemed desirable to find there.

It would have been well if Asked-of-God had examined the grounds on which this claim of infallibility rested. But this would have been to go to the bottom of the question at the start. Transitions in mental experience do not begin at the root and work up: they usually begin at some twig, work into a branch, find their way to the trunk, and ultimately reach the root only to learn that that is the point from which they ought to have started. So the writer in his departure from the old Baptist meeting-house did not begin by hammering at the corner-stone: he began up in the rafters. It would have saved him much expenditure of thought and feeling if he could have started at the base. He became conscious after a while, however, of a new mental spirit or movement. He had been accustomed to examine himself to see if *he was in the faith:* now, he began to *examine his faith* to see if it was *in him.*

In other words, a spirit of inquiry began to develop itself. It was not without prepossession, not without prejudice. We know not that such a colorless condition of mind is ever attained. But it was a spirit that was no longer willing to accept formal and conventional interpretations of truth without adequate reason. It determined to prove all things and hold fast that which is good. This is a large task to attempt. Perhaps all that we can expect to do is to prove *some* things (to our own satisfaction) and not to hold fast to things which we ought to let go.

Asked-of-God seldom or never left his own church to worship elsewhere. If circumstances compelled him to do so, he generally chose another of the same faith and order. There was little or no opportunity for him, therefore, to hear dangerous preaching. He never remembers to have heard in a Baptist pulpit at this time any heretical doctrine, save now and then a tincture of Arminianism. His contact with new and fresh thought must be established through another medium. That medium was the press. Wonderful, is it not, that subtile and painstaking art by which the curious symbolism of a multitude of black marks on a fair white page can illumine the mind with the light of new truth, quicken and unfold the affections, rouse moral energy, awaken the spiritual nature, and furnish the soul an entrance into the great realm of ideas! As he surveys his mental history, the writer finds that it was not through personal contact with individual minds, not through the hearing of the ear, but almost entirely through the medium of the printed page, that he received a new intellectual and religious impetus.

Though the young Baptist did not go to other churches when he could help it, other churches came to him. The press has proved to be an ally to the pulpit, extending the voice of the preacher to an untold distance and scattering leaves of the tree of life for the healing of the nations. It was such a leaf that came into Asked-of-God's hands. It was a sermon, published in the "Phrenological Journal," by a celebrated Brooklyn preacher, then at the height of his power. Its subject was the doctrine of conversion. The preacher maintained that conversion was not the implantation of a new nature in the soul, but simply the awakening and redirection of powers already possessed. He maintained that the Spirit of God worked through the natural constitution of the human mind. The ideas advanced concerning the organization of the mind and the operation of spiritual agencies upon it were entirely new to the reader. He had been taught, and had accepted the idea, that the regenerate soul is a new creature through the infusion of a new spiritual nature. As he studied his own experience, it did seem to him after his conversion that "all things had become new." The whole world had a changed aspect. Nevertheless, he found daily evidence that the reconstruction of his nature had been by no means complete. He looked at the lives of the converts about him. He could not see evidence of any miraculous endowment. If furnished with a new spiritual nature, why should they ever lapse again from grace? He could not account for the phenomenon of conversion on the old theory. The doctrine of the sermon he read seemed to harmonize with the facts of spiritual experience. The Spirit of God did indeed work through the mind, and not outside of it. It came with no miraculous gifts of spiritual intuition. It was the torch which kindled the soul, the sunlight and warmth which unfolded the germ in the seed to realize its hidden possibilities.

It will be seen that the heresy of the sermon was of the mildest sort. The young man read it with satisfaction. He took it to his pastor and to Brother C., expecting not agreement, but dissent. He was accustomed to affirmative nods from the oscillating head of Brother C., which, as we have already seen, served as a doctrinal indicator. For the first time in the experience of the young convert, Brother C. shook his head the other way. The sermon was not sound. But its facts and logic could not be silenced by a shake of the head, and for the first time in the four years since his conversion, Asked-of-God enjoyed the unwonted luxury of differing upon a doctrinal point from his teachers. The gap was a small one. It concerned a method rather than a result. It was an application of reason and observation to a problem which could not be settled merely by marshalling Scripture texts. It took years, however, before Asked-of-God could realize that the functions of reason and conscience in discerning truth outside of the Bible are as authoritative as when pursued within the field of exegesis, and on the foundation furnished by the written word.

XIV.

UNION AND COMMUNION.

THE old deacon, the convert's guide, had shaken his head the wrong way. The young convert had embraced a new theory about the philosophy of conversion. He had ventured to think for himself. It was a mere matter of theory. The next step was to be a marked divergence in practice.

Once more I must notice another link in the chain of circumstance. Had not a United States surgeon officially forbidden his enlistment in the navy on account of temporary ill-health, the circumstantial influence of that brief advertisement in a New York paper upon the writer's life might have been perpetually interrupted. As it was, its force was to be felt for many years to come; for it was through the kind intervention of his employers at " the place of skulls " that he was introduced to a new opportunity to repair his broken health by accepting the position of stenographer to the proprietor and chief physician of a large sanitarium in western New York; and one cool October morning he found himself at " Our Home on the Hillside," a delightful haven of rest overlooking a peaceful valley below. If considerations relating to the body had induced him to take this journey, its results were to be seen still more powerfully in his mind and heart.

Here was a little community of one hundred and fifty people, from all parts of the country, representing all shades of religious belief. Though most of them were unsound in body, few of them were unsound in theology. A large percentage were members of Christian churches. As the majority were unable to walk to town to attend denominational churches, prayers were held every morning in the chapel, a union prayer-meeting once a week, and on Sunday afternoon a service with a sermon; for once again in his life the youth had for his doctor a man who was also called to preach.

Asked-of-God went loyally at first to the Baptist church in town, and found that the zealous young pastor just hatched from a theological seminary was very fond of displaying his theological plumage. But by and by, as he made the acquaintance of the family on the hillside, he found himself irresistibly drawn toward the religious meetings which were held there. They were union meetings, communion meetings in the spiritual sense of the word. They were technically "evangelical," but sectarian differences were not obtruded. Methodists, Baptists, Presbyterians, Episcopalians, Orthodox Congregationalists, and Quakers,— all joined in the service of prayer and song. The chief physician's sermons on Sunday afternoons were marked by original eloquence and unusual power. The practical duties of life were brought into the foreground.

The body received a degree of attention worthy of its dignity as the temple of the Holy Spirit. A beautiful atmosphere of sympathy and love pervaded these meetings. They were Baptist meetings in a larger sense than any that Asked-of-God had ever attended; they were baptisms of the Spirit and of power.

The effect of this intercourse was to lift Asked-of-God out of the sectarian rut. He discovered the difference between things essential and things non-essential in Christian fellowship and in Christian life. Here were one hundred and fifty people, living together as one family, eating at the same table, sleeping under the same roof, mingling freely in their daily recreations, and joining their songs and praises in the sacred hour of worship. They were drawn together by mutual sympathies and mutual needs. A spirit of tolerance and courtesy took the place of sectarian aggressiveness. Denominational labels were not paraded. It was quite possible to associate for weeks with a Christian without knowing to what sect he belonged. The emphasis here was laid more upon character and less upon belief. Asked-of-God was still doctrinally a loyal Baptist; but here was a larger, broader, and more satisfying basis of fellowship which seemed to have some of the untainted flavor of early Christianity about it.

Why, thought the young Baptist, should not a Union Christian Church be organized on just such a broad basis as this? Why should there be half a dozen struggling, jealous, poverty-stricken churches in a place where one large church would suffice for all?

A few months later, a gradual, unexpected deepening of religious interest was manifest in the little community. It was so unlike ordinary revivals of religion that I hesitate to call it by that name. Nobody set out to bring it; no one knew how it came. It came as the dawn comes, as the spring comes. There was light in the sky and warmth in the atmosphere. The ice of formalism was melted. There was no freshet of emotion, no torrents of tears or verbiage, but a gradual blossoming of the religious life of the community. No undue excitement, no paroxysms of remorse or despair such as Asked-of-God had witnessed in other revivals, marked this silent deepening of religious interest; but its genial warmth and soul-quickening power were unmistakable.

The ministers of the various sectarian churches in town heard of this revival in the sanitarium on the hillside. It was strange to them that it should start in such a quarter. They wished some embers for their own hearth; and frequent deputations from the hillside went down to their religious meetings to carry coals from the altar. Asked-of-God recalls various missionary journeys of this sort which he made with the good physician. They were likened to Paul and Timothy as they went forth in the night, Timothy carrying a kerosene lantern and Paul a burning gospel of good-will to men. It was no little sacrifice to leave the natural warmth of the hillside prayer-meetings for the unnatural frigidity of the sectarian meetings in the valley below. Not until union meetings of the town churches were established and denominational rivalries sunken, did the Pentecostal flame from the hillside spread over the valley and kindle a spirit of unity and brotherhood. There was nothing which proved so well the genuineness of the revival as the change it wrought in the town churches themselves, so that disciples of Christ who had never thought of associating with each other were willing to meet with one accord in one place.

The little community of health-seekers on the hillside had been held together religiously by an invisible bond. It seemed somewhat perilous to attempt to make the union an organic one. Could this heterogeneous band of Methodists, Baptists, Presbyterians, Episcopalians, Quakers, Congregationalists, and, if I mistake not, one or two Unitarians and Universalists, be brought together on a common platform of religious faith? The attempt was made. The conditions were favorable. The genial revival which preceded had tempered all hearts with charity and kindliness. The unity of the spirit had created a bond of peace.

The constitution and covenant of that little union church are before me. The opening articles declare the name to be "The Church of Christ," and adopt the Congregational order for its government. The pastor, four deacons, and the church clerk constitute its officers. The object of the church is stated to be "to consolidate and make effective the Christian life of this community for its own growth, for the conversion of others, and to work with and upon other Christian churches." The most interesting and important articles are those relating to membership : —

ART. 7. — All who make open confession of faith in Christ and give credible evidence of Christian life are entitled to become members of this church by a vote of a majority of the church present, and on signing the confession of faith.

CONFESSION OF FAITH.

We hereby confess our faith in Jesus Christ as our all-sufficient and only Saviour from sin and its condemnation, and cheerfully take him to be our supreme Lord and Master, who himself hath said, "Except a man be born again, he cannot enter the kingdom of God."

We also accept the Bible as a revelation of God's will to man, and hereby acknowledge our obligation and express our purpose to live according to its teachings, especially as embodied in its great law, as declared by Christ, namely, "Thou shalt love the Lord thy God with all thy heart and with all thy soul and with all thy strength and with all thy mind, and thy neighbor as thyself."

This confession of faith must be judged, not by its adequacy for any one element in the church, but by its adequacy for all. No Trinity, no doctrine of election, no scheme of everlasting punishment, no vicarious atonement, no infallible Bible, was either affirmed or denied. Yet these omissions did not impair the vitality of the union. There was another significant article in the constitution of the church: —

ART. 10. — The Lord's Supper and the rite of baptism are considered by this church as appropriate Christian ordinances, which should be accepted by all Christians as great helps to the growth of the divine life in their souls; but no person or persons who cannot accept either or both as such, yet who give satisfactory evidence to this church that they have been accepted of Christ and are his dear children, shall, by reason of their want of conformity to these ordinances, be excluded from membership and fellowship herein.

This article was the bridge that spanned the chasm between the Quaker and the close-communion Baptist.

What would old Brother C. have said of it? But Asked-of-God had come under the benediction of a broader and more tolerant Christian influence; and after he had become one of the fifty who signed the confession on New Year's day, when the church was formed, he wrote in his journal, "I rejoice to see a church organized on such a broad platform, and heartily wish that every church in the land were as catholic as this."

Two weeks later, he received a letter of criticism, twenty-four pages in length, from a Baptist friend at home, to whom he had communicated his action.

There are few things fresher or sweeter in the memory of Asked-of-God than the hallowed association which he formed with this Church of Christ, and the rich and fruitful affections which sanctified it. Among these pictures of memory there looms up one of a beautiful summer afternoon. A sweet peace was at the heart of Nature. It was easy to commune with the Eternal; the veil of the temple seemed transparent to a loving, God-seeking heart. As the shadows lengthened in the afternoon, and the glory of the departing day was softened into a more mysterious light, the little band of Christians gathered in the hall, which to them was a sanctuary consecrated by their vows and prayers, and partook together of the eucharistic feast, — a feast of gratitude, aspiration, and love. It was the first time Asked-of-God had ever sat at the table of the Lord outside of a Baptist church. Once he would have deemed it disloyal to Christ to eat at that table with an unbaptized Christian, the only valid baptism in his mind being baptism by immersion. Now, it seemed disloyal not to do so. He had studied his Bible, and failed to find any evidence that baptism was to be the doorway to the Lord's table. Still more, however, he had learned to believe in the baptism of the Holy Ghost and in the communion of saints.

This act of drinking from the same cup and eating from the same loaf in a religious service with a band of Christians of all sects and beliefs would have been enough upon which to base an action for his expulsion from the old Baptist church at home. But before that action was taken, the conscientious brethren who began it were to have still other grounds for the painful step.

XV.

SUNDAY OBSERVANCE.

WHEN Asked-of-God went from the sanitarium in western New York, leaving the union church behind him, he felt that his mental and sympathetic life had been perceptibly broadened. The world had a different aspect. He saw things in new relations. Let us hope that he was more charitable than when he went there. He had broken the "close-communion" fetters which previously bound him. He recalls now how his mother writhed under those manacles.

"To think," she once said to the boy, when visiting her brother who was a Presbyterian, "that I cannot eat the Lord's Supper with my own beloved brother, when we sit together in the same pew!"

Her conscience compelled her to refuse the elements when the good Presbyterian deacon offered them, but her heart bled under the strain. Her loyalty to the established usages of her church and the assumption that immersion was a necessary preparation for the Lord's Supper were the only reasons she could offer against the larger claims of love and fellowship.

Other Christian denominations that require baptism before admitting to the Lord's Supper cannot consistently reproach the Baptists for doing the same thing, though other denominations are less rigid in insisting on a certain form of the preparatory rite. In England, our Baptist brethren have almost entirely given up the close-communion practice. Few have uttered more stirring words against it than Robert Hall and Mr. Spurgeon.

On the whole subject of ritualistic observances, Asked-of-God had become more tolerant. He still clung to immersion as the most beautiful and significant form of baptism, but he no longer rested the value of the service upon the amount of water used. Infant baptism he did not find taught in the New Testament, and has never found it there since, but regards it as a beautiful and profitable service for parents to consecrate their children to God.

His views of Sabbath observance had also suffered a great change. They had been distinguished by remarkable rigor. So strict had he been, a few years before, that he would not ride in a street car, nor cross the river in a ferry-boat, nor buy a newspaper, nor conduct any commercial transaction on Sunday. The line of his reading on that day was narrowly religious. Such Sabbaths might have been a severe burden to him, if he had not usually filled them up with so much active work for the salvation of souls. One Sunday, while Asked-of-God was still at the sanitarium, a good Baptist sister from Philadelphia gave him a copy of a paper she had received, which contained a sermon by the Rev. William Henry Furness, D.D., of that city. It was on the subject of Sabbath observance.

If I mistake not, it was entitled "The Sabbath made for Man." As the sermon had to be returned, Asked-of-God could not preserve the paper as he would gladly have done; but he preserved something better. He preserved the spirit of the discourse, its argument and its conclusions. He had not before heard of the author, and read the discourse without prejudice; but it was clear, rational, and liberal in its tone. It made the Christian Sabbath an instrument, not an end; a large, free day; a day for rest and invigoration, for growth and culture. It sanctioned no lawless, boisterous, intemperate desecration, but pleaded for larger liberty and a more rational employment of Sunday rest.

This is another example of the way in which the press may act as an ally to the pulpit. Here was a fugitive sermon from a distant city, which had casually fallen into his hands. It had cracked the burr of the old superstitions, removed the husk, but left the meat inside. The good Baptist sister was a little alarmed when she discovered the influence that this sermon had exerted. It must be said, however, that, in giving up the old rigid Puritanic Sunday, Asked-of-God surrendered it wholly from principle. He did not drop into lax practices, and then accommodate his principles to them, nor did he form conclusions without sifting evidence and weighing argument.

But old associations remain even when intellectual convictions have been changed. Asked-of-God still loves the quietude and simplicity of the Puritan Sabbath. He has never become reconciled to the French and German

Sunday, in which recreation so largely supplants worship. With the lapse of years, he no longer finds it "wicked" to listen on Sunday to strains from inspired composers, which are not put down in the church music-books. He no longer finds it "wicked" to have the public libraries or the Art Museum open on that day. When he remembers the pale faces of the men who toiled for fifty-nine hours a week in the great manufacturing establishment where so much of his boyhood was spent, he finds it no robbery of God to make accessible to them suburban parks where they may hear the birds sing and fill their lungs with the freshness of fragrant breezes. He would no longer stop the boats and the horse-cars or the Sunday trains.

Yet let not the reaction from the Puritan Sabbath go too far. That day was hooped and barred with many restrictions. Break the hoops and the bars, but do not destroy the day itself. Let necessary labor be done, but let not Sunday be surrendered to the insatiate hunger of commerce and trade. Sunday must not be put into the market, and sold at its money value. The moral, intellectual, and spiritual opportunities of the day are of far more worth to the workingman than the wages he could command by laboring habitually on that day. To Asked-of-God, the ideal way of keeping the Sabbath is to devote a portion of the time to the public worship of God, a portion to mental invigoration and the delights of home or the enjoyment of Nature, and a portion to the religious education of youth and the improvement of society.

The unfortunate habit which is too prevalent of abandoning Sunday worship is largely a reaction, no doubt, from the stern rigor of the old Puritan method. The extreme effects of such reaction cannot be corrected by trying to put up the old fences and bars. A more effective way will be to teach men, in whatever way they keep the day, to keep it unto the Lord. The day is a priceless legacy, not to be squandered in vain frivolities or habitual self-indulgence. It is a time for rest, worship, aspiration, love, and earnest service for humanity. Who has paid a higher tribute to the Sabbath than did Emerson in his famous address at Cambridge forty-seven years ago? —

Two inestimable advantages Christianity has given us: first, the Sabbath, the jubilee of the whole world, whose light dawns welcome alike into the closet of the philosopher, into the garret of toil, and into prison cells, and everywhere suggests, even to the vile, the dignity of spiritual being. Let it stand forevermore, — a temple which new love, new faith, new sight, shall restore to more than its first splendor to mankind.

XVI.

AN EFFECTIVE SERMON.

ASKED-OF-GOD'S change of views on the Sabbath question permitted him to take a position as reporter on a leading New York daily. His Sunday duties required him to attend, from week to week, a great variety of churches. Sometimes he reported Mr. Beecher in the morning and Archbishop McCloskey in the evening. The next Sunday perhaps he found himself worshipping in a Methodist church in the morning and in an Episcopal church in the evening. Sometimes he was assigned to a meeting of the Spiritualists, and took purported revelations from the other world. There was hardly a sect or denomination which did not secure his services in the course of the year. This roving life was quite in contrast to his previous habit of close adhesion to a single church. He did not altogether enjoy being a religious tramp. He missed the kindly associations which church life develops. He longed to unite his efforts with other earnest workers in the cause of religion and morality. The opportunity finally came. The impulse of that little short-hand advertisement was still propagated. He was summoned to Washington as private secretary to one of the members of the Cabinet. Henceforth he was relieved from the necessity of attending different churches to satisfy the vague spiritual wants of a daily paper.

He determined, first of all, to find some practical religious work in which he could engage from Sunday to Sunday. The war had just closed. There were thousands of negroes in the District under the care of the Freedman's Bureau. About this time Asked-of-God, like the Apostle Peter, had begun to lead about a wife. He had not only found his life at the sanitarium, but had doubled it. He and his wife resolved to do what they could for this neglected race. On the first Sunday after their arrival in the national capital they set out to find some mission school in which their services would be welcome. They visited two, only to find that they had all the teachers they needed. The third application was more successful. They were gladly received, and began their work of instruction in the old barracks on Seventh Street, near the Boundary. The association thus formed proved to be one of great value. It opened not only a welcome opportunity to help a needy people, but it brought Asked-of-God and his companion into association with warm and earnest Christian hearts. Nearly all the members of that little band have since been scattered the country over, but some of the ties thus formed have remained unbroken to the present day.

Asked-of-God also joined the Young Men's Christian Association. His connection with an "evangelical" church permitted him to become an active member of that organization, and he was soon elected one of its officers. It opened to him a field of educational and practical work, which he enjoyed. He met here Christians of all denominations except Unitarians, Universalists, and Swedenborgians, who were excluded from active membership.

I am convinced that he was right, in this stage of his development, in seeking opportunities for moral and religious effort. It is unwise for young men who are encountering the intellectual or ethical difficulties of the current theology to withdraw from practical moral and religious work. Speculation is not dangerous so long as it is theoretical. It becomes baneful when it paralyzes the moral energies. There were a good many things that Asked-of-God could not settle in his own mind, but of one thing he was sure, — that he had certain duties which he owed to his fellow-men. He determined then and there to do what he could for the enlightenment and elevation of humanity.

The connection he formed at the mission school and at the Association largely supplied the place of an active membership with any of the city churches. Nevertheless he was disposed to unite with a church, provided he could find one which was congenial. He was still a member of the old Baptist church in New York, into whose fellowship he had been baptized. He was also a member of the union church described in a previous chapter, and entitled to a letter of dismission from it which would admit him to an Orthodox Congregational church. He did not feel authorized, however, to use either of these keys to open a church door. The love of the old Baptist nest was still strong in his heart. When he determined to seek a regular place of worship, he began by attending one of the most prominent Baptist churches in the city. Unfortunately, the minister chewed tobacco. The minister under whom he had been converted and by whom he had been baptized had been addicted to the same habit. Perhaps Asked-of-God associated it with a violent form of Calvinism. Experience has taught him the incorrectness of this deduction. Arminians and Liberals, he has discovered, may also roll the cud as a sweet morsel under their tongues. He did not feel, however, like sitting again from Sunday to Sunday under the ministrations of a man who could not preach effectively without filling his mouth with a noxious weed. He admits his intolerance. Possibly the words which came from the speaker's mouth confirmed the hearer's prejudice against its contents.

The next Sunday, he and his wife attended another Baptist church. The preacher was known as one of the most prominent, though not the most popular, in the city. He had two hearers that evening who came with reasonable expectations of hearing a good sermon. They were wofully disappointed. His subject was the unpardonable sin. The text was taken from the words of Jesus concerning blasphemy against the Holy Ghost, and the words of 1 John v. 16: "There is a sin unto death: I do not say that he shall pray for it." The preacher stated that the unpardonable sin had been committed in days that were passed, and might be committed in the present. Blasphemy he defined as "a malicious reviling of God, a total rejection of Christ, persistent resistance of the Holy Ghost, and an animosity toward the gospel."

With astonishing and cold-blooded particularity, he then gave two instances in which he believed the unpardonable sin had been committed. One was that of an old man in New England. The minister called upon him on one occasion. The old man drew him aside, and earnestly begged him to give his attention to his children, saying that for himself he had too long resisted the gospel; he was beyond hope; he had sinned against the Holy Ghost, there was no salvation for him. He died in this belief. Another was the case of a woman who had a similar feeling. Her husband had died. She believed he had gone to hell, and wanted to go there with him. The preacher did not hesitate to assure his audience of his belief that these persons had not only died without hope, but without salvation. He represented it as quite possible that some one in the audience before him had committed that sin. It was a sin beyond praying for.

Asked-of-God was filled with indignation. The cool presumption of the speaker amazed him. That a minister of Jesus Christ could stand in the pulpit and speak in this mechanical, heartless way, was inexplicable, except on the ground that he did not believe the terrible doctrine he was preaching. If he had had a tithe of the zeal of the colored preacher whom Asked-of-God had heard in the morning, and who seemed to be ready to rush into the pit to save his hearers from its flames, the preacher would have commanded the respect due to sincere convictions and burning zeal. He was preaching a flaming hell, yet he himself was as cool as an iceberg.

The preacher closed his sermon with a prayer that his hearers might be led to the truth. But there were two present who were inclined to believe that if the prayer was granted, none of his hearers would accept the heartless form of fatalism which he had been preaching to them.

As he reflected upon the stories which the minister had so coldly related, Asked-of-God drew from them quite a different lesson. There was an element of heroism shining through that black despondency. The man who believed he was going to hell was not entirely absorbed in the thought of his own horrible destiny. His love for his children gleamed through his grim despair. He would have *them* saved, if he could not be saved himself. The woman was yet more devoted. Her husband, she felt sure, had gone to hell. With a sweet unselfishness, she gave up all desire for the joys of heaven that she might share his woe with him. This divine heroism had wholly escaped the attention of this Christian minister.

Asked-of-God's whole soul rebelled with all its energy against the caricature of God which had been presented to him. It was not the first time that he had heard the cruelty and injustice of God preached from the pulpit, but he had never heard it presented in quite such a frigid and merciless way. He had been taught in Sunday-school and church that the doctrine was true, and had believed it with fear and trembling, because he was too young to examine the evidence of its truth. He now became impressed with the evidence of its falsity. He went out from that church believing that the doctrine of the endless damnation of human souls is a libel upon the character of a just and merciful God. He had not been forced to this conclusion in a Universalist Church; he had reached it in a Baptist meeting-house. There was poetic justice in this. It was in a Baptist meeting-house that he had first heard this doctrine presented with terrifying power. He had shuddered in his seat in his youthful days as the terrors of hell had been depicted by a man who seemed to believe in the reality of the fictions he was describing; and it was in a Baptist meeting-house that a cold and spiritless speaker had roused him to moral indignation by the empty ring of his gospel of despair. It is just such preaching as this that has made many converts to Universalism, and driven others into open hostility to every form of Christianity.

Asked-of-God had taken another important step. He henceforth refused to believe that God would condemn to everlasting punishment the greater portion of the human race, simply to satisfy his own inordinate thirst for an unhallowed glory. He refused to believe that God would consign men to an endless hell simply because they could not believe that he was the cruel and unrighteous being that men had painted him. He refused to believe that subscription to any form of doctrine, held by any church, was to fix the final destiny of a man for untold ages. He refused to believe that God does not possess the most ordinary attributes of justice and mercy which he has enjoined upon his creatures.

He refused to believe these things only that he might believe something better. It was a joy to his soul to feel that God was not the cruel and jealous despot that theology had made him. He rejoiced in the loving fatherhood of God which Jesus had so tenderly preached. He found rest and satisfaction in feeling that the law of the divine action was not arbitrary or capricious, but the offspring of eternal wisdom, justice, and love. It was a great satisfaction to believe that the moral laws which operate in this life are to operate in the next. The law of retribution was not abrogated. It achieved a new and a diviner force. Its synonyme was, "Whatsoever a man soweth, that shall he also reap."

XVII.

THREE LUMINOUS BOOKS.

THE library of the State Department at Washington was exceptionally good for its size. Asked-of-God counted it a bit of good fortune that his desk was situated in one of its alcoves. A short flight of stairs communicated with Mr. Seward's room below. From time to time, his phonographic pencil was summoned by the Secretary of State to take down utterances which have been carefully preserved in our diplomatic history. Sometimes it was page after page of a despatch to some foreign minister, growing out of the recent and complicated issues of the war. The thought which trickled from his pencil found its way to the Court of England or the Court of France, or perhaps was exiled to the Russian capital. Sometimes it was advice or direction to a remote consul, then a communication for Congress, or a message to go to that body with the signature of the President. There was nothing provincial or narrow in this work. It dealt with large political and human relations. It gave new breadth and scope to the mind, and awakened interest in broad and independent historical study. The library, too, afforded much delight. There was one alcove in which at least one reader loved to browse. It was devoted mainly to the old English preachers. Here for the first time he made the acquaintance of South, Jeremy Taylor, and Tillotson. South allured by his wit, Taylor charmed by the poetry of his style. With from six to sixteen Greek and Latin quotations on a page, however, his sermons were like a sword, the hilt of which was richly set with borrowed jewels. It was in the simplicity, clearness, and moral power of Tillotson that Asked-of-God took special delight. There was little that was controversial in his sermons. They furnished rich food for the moral and religious life.

One day, however, the reader was attracted by another series of books in the same alcove. They were more modern in their aspect. One of them was entitled "Ten Sermons on Religion." The author was Theodore Parker. The discovery at first awakened no special interest. The reader was conscious of a strong prejudice against the author, whom he regarded as an out-and-out infidel. To be sure, he had never read a line of his works; but the most bitter prejudices are often founded upon ignorance or misrepresentation. He ventured, however, to read a page or two in this volume. His interest was quickly kindled. The writer was surely not the man he had taken him to be. With great delight, he read through the sermon on "Conscious Religion as a Source of Joy;" another on "Conscious Religion as a Source of Strength;" a third on "The Culture of the Religious Powers." These sermons seemed to contain in themselves the qualities of joy, strength, and culture by which they were entitled. It was not the literary style which charmed the reader; it was the richness, beauty, and strength of the religious sentiment they contained. It is not too much to say that he had always been led to suppose that Theodore Parker was a bad and dangerous man. But there was a quality in his "infidelity" of which the reader had never dreamed. It was marked by a rational tone, animated by an earnest and practical aim, and pervaded by a deep and strong spirit of religious trust. The reader still preserved the Puritanic habit of keeping a diary. When he had finished these discourses, he wrote in it a humble confession of the wrong he had done Mr. Parker, and registered a vow never to hear him accused of irreligion without coming to his defence.

He found much, to be sure, in the writings of Parker that he was not wholly prepared to accept. They were colored with a strong individuality. His marked originality sometimes surprised more than it satisfied. There was an audacity which was not always tender of other people's prejudices. But there was something inspiring in his fearless honesty, in the height and depth of his theism, and in the glow of his vision as he looked out upon the future life. When Asked-of-God laid down the volume of the "Ten Sermons on Religion," he was glad he knew Theodore Parker as he was, not merely as he had supposed him to be.

In Parker's prayers, he found a new and nourishing aspect of the spirit of devotion. He took them home, and drank freely from this fountain of sweet and manly piety. To assure himself that these prayers were fitted to satisfy universal spiritual needs, he tried an interesting experiment. It was his custom to offer or read a prayer at the family devotions in the morning. An elderly orthodox lady, whose piety exhaled as sweetly from her nature as fragrance from a flower, was spending a few weeks under his roof. She still held strongly to features of the orthodox creed which her host had come strongly to doubt, but her soul was open toward God. One morning, Asked-of-God read without warning a prayer of Theodore Parker. The next morning, he read another.

"What a beautiful prayer!" said the old lady. Asked-of-God handed her the volume. Her surprise was beyond measure when she learned that its author was the arch-heretic.

For one who was just emerging from the darkness of the old theology into the twilight of Liberal Christianity, Theodore Parker's works may seem to have been rather strong meat. But Asked-of-God had as yet no guide in this period of mental transition. He read Parker's works first, simply because they came in his way. Channing was the natural correlative to the works of Parker. He was soon found in the same library, and read with equal delight. Here were luminous and rational expositions of moral and spiritual relations, and like Parker's pervaded with a deep human interest and uttered without cant.

The writer counts it as his good fortune that he made the acquaintance of these authors so nearly at the same time. The positions they represented seemed widely different in many respects; but the ethical and practical earnestness of their tone and the deep religious spirit which they both exhibited were indications of a unity beneath diversity.

One afternoon, while walking on Pennsylvania Avenue, Asked-of-God entered a familiar second-hand bookstore. Here on its dusty shelves, amid a luxurious growth of weeds and thorns, might be found occasionally some of the sweetest flowers of literature. What lover of books has not gathered honey for his hive from such a field! It was not history, politics, or art, but a volume of sermons which most attracted the explorer's attention. It was entitled "The Christian Body and Form," by C. A. Bartol, pastor of the West Church, Boston. The reader knew nothing of the West Church, Boston, or its pastor,— whether the church was Baptist, Methodist, Episcopalian, or, what was least suspected at the time, Unitarian. He took it up absolutely without prejudice. After reading a few pages, he bought the book, took it home, and read it aloud. Without controversy, great was the mystery of its godliness. It was original in style, beautifully poetic, and handled spiritual themes with reverence and delicacy. From the symbol it unfolded the reality. It was not until after the volume had been read that it was learned that the writer of this charming book was an "Independent Congregational" minister in Boston, settled over a Unitarian church.

By sheer good fortune, with that measure of credit only

which belongs to the hungry mind, Asked-of-God had stumbled on three Unitarian books. No one had placed them in his hands. He had found them, and made them his own. It was fortunate, perhaps, that he learned to know something of the devotional and religious side of Unitarianism before he came in direct contact with its controversial side. Unitarianism, as Asked-of-God approached it, was anything but negative in its character. He had read these books with the same hunger that he had read Taylor and Tillotson. They had refreshed and strengthened his soul. He felt called upon again to examine the foundation of his own beliefs. As yet, he had heard no Unitarian preaching, nor was he acquainted with any Unitarian layman. Yet, under the roof of the State Department, occupying an honored and important position, was a prominent member of the Unitarian church at Washington. A casual comparison of views, on a journey which they made together with the Secretary of State, led to the discovery of a mutual sympathy in matters of religion. A few days after, this Unitarian brother kindly gave to his companion a bundle of tracts dealing with some prominent aspects of Unitarian belief. They were most of them based upon the Bible as the source of authority in such appeals. With the old Baptist instinct for Scriptural authority, Asked-of-God turned to that book in the spirit of the Bereans, "who were more noble than those in Thessalonica, in that they received the Word with all readiness of mind, and searched the Scriptures daily whether those things were so."

XVIII.

SEARCHING THE BIBLE, AND WHAT CAME OF IT.

THERE is a familiar story of an old woman who, on receiving a visit from her pastor, took down the family Bible from a shelf to enjoy the satisfaction of hearing him read the sacred Word. She broke forth into an unguarded exclamation of surprise and gratification on discovering within the book the spectacles which she had lost six months before. Most people may have more success than this old lady in concealing their want of familiarity with the Bible, but nearly every one has a special pair of spectacles through which he views it. When Asked-of-God opened his Bible again, he did not find, however, the same spectacles that he had used a few years before. I will not venture to say that he had none whatever. It is not quite possible for one who has had any Christian training to read the Bible with precisely the same impartiality as a cultivated and intelligent heathen — such as Rammohun Roy, for instance — might read it for the first time. The prejudices of the writer, so far as he had any, were, on the side of his education, wholly in favor of the Calvinistic system. But in this fresh examination his spectacles were, so far as he could make them, optically achromatic. He did not bring learning or genius to its interpretation; but this I can say, that no one ever read the Bible in a spirit of more absolute sincerity. It still seemed to him as if a special divine revelation glowed from its pages. Once more he turned to the Epistle of James, and read, "If any of you lack wisdom, let him ask of God, that giveth to all men liberally, and upbraideth not; and it shall be given him." He read the Bible "on his knees."

The genuineness of these books he did not question; he did not doubt the truthfulness of their writers. He did not ask how these books had been put together. There was a whole line of antecedent historical study which he ought to have taken up, but he did not understand the need of it at that time. He took the Bible as it was.

He had been confronted with certain propositions and statements by Unitarian authors. They were legible and rational on their face. He simply went to the Bible to see if they were true. He read the New Testament through in the English, and studied debatable passages in the Greek. Great was his surprise to find that the Bible did not contain certain things which he had always supposed were taught in its pages. In his early youth, he had never fully investigated the Bible proofs of the Trinity and of the nature of Jesus Christ. He had always taken these for granted in the doctrinal form presented to him. He had gone to the Bible rather as a quiver of Calvinistic texts in his old battle with Arminianism. These he had found most plentiful in the Epistles of Paul. But now he turned first and foremost to the Gospels. Who was this Jesus who had come into the world? What did he say for himself? What message did he bring to needy humanity? How did he live and how did he die? What was the grand lesson of his life? These were pressing questions.

What did this earnest student find in the Bible? Rather let me ask, first of all, what he did *not* find there. *He did not find the doctrine of the Trinity taught in any part, nor implied in the Bible as a whole.*

It was not in the Old Testament. This was purely a monotheistic book. He was surprised, almost confounded, not to find it in the New. How should he answer this Unitarian challenge? He turned for help to Hitchcock's "New and Complete Analysis of the Holy Bible," or the whole of the Old and New Testaments arranged according to subjects. Under the head of the doctrine of the Trinity, he found one passage under which the doctrine was said to be "*foreshadowed*" (Genesis i. 26): "And God said, Let us make man in our image, after our likeness; and let them have dominion over the fish of the sea, and over the fowl of the air, and over the cattle, and over all the earth, and over every creeping thing that creepeth upon the earth." A strange foreshadowing of the doctrine of the Trinity! And this the only passage in the Old Testament!

He turned to the references in the New Testament. There were two passages in which it was said to be "hinted at," — Ephesians ii. 18: "For through him we both have access by one Spirit [or, as the Revised Version now has it, "*in* one Spirit"] unto the Father." There was no "hint" of personality in the "spirit" here, any more than there was in the words of Jesus in John iv. 24, that "God is a spirit, and they that worship him must worship him in spirit and in truth." A feeble hint this on which to build Christian tritheism!

Another hint adduced was the similar passage in Ephesians ii. 22, "In whom ye also are builded together for an habitation of God through the Spirit," which is no more trinitarian than the preceding.

For the third hint of the doctrine, the reader was referred to Ephesians iv. 4–6: "There is one body and one Spirit, even as ye are called in one hope of your calling; one Lord, one faith, one baptism, one God and Father of all, who is above all, and through all, and in you all." This passage proved Paul to be an out-and-out monotheist, if it proved anything. Not the feeblest adumbration of the Trinity here.

But there were still three passages given in which the doctrine was said to be "*implied*." One of these was the benediction in 2 Corinthians xiii. 14: "The grace of the Lord Jesus Christ, and the love of God, and the communion of the Holy Ghost, be with you all." The form of the Trinity was given here, but not the doctrine itself. It was a benediction, not a creed. There was a tender beauty in this blessing which invoked "the grace of the Lord Jesus Christ" and that love of God which can only be realized through communion with the divine Spirit. The baptismal formula in Matthew xxviii. 19 is of similar character.

There was another passage referred to (1 Peter i. 2), in which God and Jesus and the Spirit were mentioned; but there was no Trinity here.

One more passage was given in the "Complete Analysis" (1 John v. 7): "For there are three that bear record in heaven, the Father, the Word, and the Holy Ghost: and these three are one." This last passage at first staggered Asked-of-God not a little; but a note at the bottom of the page informed him that these words "are wanting in the best manuscripts, like the Sinaitic and the Vatican, as also in most of the ancient versions, and are now generally considered spurious." When he turned to the version of the New Testament made under the auspices of his Baptist brethren, he found that they had had the candor and scholarship to omit this verse, as it has since been omitted in the Revised Version.

Leaving out this well-known spurious passage, what was left to support the doctrine of the Trinity? Only a "hint," a "foreshadowing," and an "implication." The insertion of the spurious passage in the book of John was changed from a proof to a strong evidence against the doctrine. It was inserted to supply a proof which was lacking.

I have before me some of the notes which Asked-of-God made at the time he pursued this investigation. They are still entirely legible. One of them is an extract from Neander, in which he says concerning the Trinity: —

This doctrine does not strictly belong to the fundamental articles of the Christian faith, as appears sufficiently evident from the fact that it is expressly held forth by no one particular passage of the New Testament. For the only one in which it is contained, the passage relating to the three that bear record (1 John v. 7), is undoubtedly spurious, and in its ungenuine shape testifies to the fact how foreign such a collocation is from the style of the New Testament Scriptures. We find in the New Testament no other fundamental article than that of which the Apostle Paul says, "Other foundation can no man lay than that is laid," — the annunciation of Jesus Christ as the Messiah.

Asked-of-God turned from this examination therefore with the distinct conviction that the doctrine of the Trinity is not taught in the Bible.

As for the logical argument, he found little in favor of the hair-splitting discussions of the old theologians. The doctrine as presented in the creeds was not so much a mystery as a contradiction; and the student jotted down in his notes: " A doctrine that contains two propositions, one of which contradicts the other, should hardly be made a reason for damning those who have the temerity to reject it." The Athanasian creed lays down a certain number of propositions in regard to the Trinity. Whoever would be saved must accept these propositions, but it is safe to say that no one ever succeeded in mentally grasping them. As Dr. James Freeman Clarke truly says, "The Orthodox ask us to believe a proposition which they are unable intelligently to express;" and he adds with much force, "The heaviest charge against the church doctrine of the Trinity is that, driven to despair by these difficulties, it has at last made Orthodoxy consist, not in any sound belief, but only in sound phrases. It is not *believing* anything, but *saying* something which now makes a man orthodox. If you will only use the word 'trinity' in any sense, if you will call Christ God in any sense, you are orthodox."

In the cloudy metaphysics of the Schoolmen, the doctrine of the Trinity was but an evaporated tritheism. It had in it no practical spiritual power. It was a metaphysical attempt to analyze and determine the constituent proportions of the Deity. It was an infusion of Greek gnosticism into Christianity.

And yet, as Asked-of-God turned to the Bible, though he did not find the Trinity there, he found a representation of God in his relations to humanity which was helpful and beautiful. He still believed in the Father, and in the Son, and in the manifestation of the Holy Spirit in the world. To show just what his belief was, I am tempted to quote from a letter which he wrote at this time to a friend. As I read it over, I am reminded that it was not intended for print at the time it was written, and that it might have been better worded, — that it was too much encumbered with theological phrases; but I give it as it is to show the attitude of mind it represented: —

"Do you not then," you may ask, "believe in the Father, the Son, and the Holy Ghost?" Most assuredly. They are terms that have as deep a significance and as definite an application in the spiritual and superhuman world as the terms "father" and "son" and "spirit" have in the human world. I do believe in God the Father, — or, as Theodore Parker tenderly expresses it, " the Infinite Mother." He is one that my soul prays and longs after. My head finds rest in the bosom of his love. Its doubts and fears are quieted when it receives his constant caress. He watches over me, cares for me, clothes me, feeds me, talks with me, instructs, guides, and supports me. He is sorrowful when I sin, and chastens me only to correct and improve. I am constantly environed by his mercies and nourished by his grace. How can I say I believe not in the Father, when more than any other fact in the universe he impresses my consciousness, which he has made alive with susceptibility to his presence; when he has hollowed out a chamber of longing in my soul, a yearning, which only he can fill!

I believe in Christ the Son, as " God with us ; " as " God manifest in the flesh ; " as one who was one with God as we may be one with Christ and one with God, if we follow in his footsteps. I believe in Christ the Son as the most human and yet the most divine presentation of God's love that the world has ever seen. I accept him for all that he offers himself, as the dearly beloved Son of the Father, who came to us as the Way and the Truth and the Life.

I believe in the Holy Spirit, as a constant emanation from God ; as the outflow of his being which informs the world with his presence, which is not only the principle of all animal life, but the principle of spiritual and eternal life. I believe that men need to be quickened by this Spirit into spiritual newness and energy ; that without God's Spirit we cannot enter into his kingdom.

I believe in this trinity of manifestations, and, declaring the distinct individuality of the Father and the Son, I believe in their entire unity, — that unity of spirit, aim, purpose, which transcends the unity of matter and substance, and reveals God as the Great Heart of the Universe, with whose pulse all who reverence and obey him must beat in unison. That Christ lived a spotless, blameless life, was because of his oneness with the Father. The will of God was his single aim, his meat and his drink. He was at one with him, and the great object of his life was that we might be at one with God also.

I assert, not that God is *confined to a trinity in his manifestations, rather that he is manifold in his presentations of himself.* But our highest and sweetest conceptions of him, our highest knowledge of him, are derived from that ever blessed trinity in which he has revealed himself to us, — the Father, Son, and Holy Spirit.

This is an all-sufficient revelation of himself, — sufficient to banish the darkness of atheism, and light the world with the reality of his presence; sufficient to bring us all into a true knowledge of him whom to know aright is life eternal.

XIX.

WHAT THINK YE OF CHRIST?

ASKED-OF-GOD could not find that the doctrine of the Trinity was taught in the New Testament. There was another question which now loomed up before him. It was, "What think ye of Christ?" In framing his answer he determined, first of all, to study the words of Jesus concerning himself. He would then diligently study the words of his disciples about him.

It is somewhat hazardous, years after we have pursued any special historical or critical study, or experienced any great change in belief, to recall from memory the various steps by which it was reached. But in this record there is no danger of mistake, for Asked-of-God had the habit of writing down in detail the results of his investigations. I have before me a somewhat formidable document, covering fifty-eight pages of foolscap, in which he carefully recorded the conclusions he reached, and embodied them in a letter to a Baptist friend. It will show better the state of the inquirer's mind after this examination, if I quote portions of his words instead of giving my own.

Perhaps it is less important that I should give all the evidence on which Asked-of-God founded his conclusions than that I should let the reader look into his brain and heart through the windows which this unpublished treatise affords. The paper possesses more unity of structure than might appear from these detached and dismembered paragraphs.

A NATURAL INQUIRY.

Considerable diversity of opinion is permitted in regard to the Trinity, without suspicion of one's orthodoxy; but Christ's absolute divinity is guarded with jealous and vigilant care. Yet there would seem to be nothing more legitimate or natural than the question, "Who was Christ?" No character in history may excite such admiration, wonder, and reverential inquiry. It was the purpose of Christ to challenge criticism and investigation. He came to "bear witness to the truth," and knew that his witness was true. He rebuked not the wonder questions which his life excited. It was natural in his age that his life should beget inquiry. That inquiry has been projected for centuries. The great mass of the Church, in his day, were content with his own answer to the question of his origin and nature. But, as the question has rolled to us down the centuries, it has gathered up a multitude of answers that Jesus never made, but that men have made for him. And when we come to look at our doctrine to-day, piled up on the history of eighteen centuries, we find that we have elected Jesus to a position which he never claimed. We have made him God instead of God's well-beloved Son. Within the pale of Orthodoxy, that is almost the only conclusion that is admitted. This conclusion is nailed up for acceptance, but scarcely for investigation.

THE GOSPEL CHRIST.

As a Baptist, your Bible is Supreme Court in theology. With me, it is not the only source of appeal, but a very important one; and you may have more respect for my views, when I tell you that I am willing to go to that source of authority to test them. No reading of mine has contributed more to change my views on the subject of the Trinity and the nature of Christ than a thorough reading of the New Testament in the original. I found that the gospel Christ was different from the theologic Christ. I was surprised to find what an amount of dogma had been hung upon verbal and inferential pegs, and how easily, in the course of time, a hypothesis could be condensed into a fact or a fact turned into a hypothesis. Thus, the idea of Christ, which I have quoted from the Assembly Catechism, is that " two whole, perfect, and distinct natures, the Godhead and the manhood, were inseparably joined together in one person, which person is very God and very man." Yet it would be hard to find anything in the sayings of Christ concerning himself which show that he was what this represents him to be, and difficult to find its equivalent anywhere in the New Testament. That book avoids the metaphysics, or philosophy, of Christ's nature. It prefers a natural definition of him, a definition so simple that a child can understand it: he was the *Son of God*. This is plain enough for the child, but too plain for the catechists who wish to teach it. That which is clear must be mystified, the plain must be ex-plained, and the simple must be complicated before it can be said to be a *sound* theological statement.

SCRIPTURE TESTIMONY.

Let us look at some of the Scripture testimony concerning Jesus, which I think conclusively states his *derivation from* and *subordination to* God.

In the first place, notice the emphasis which is laid on his being the Son of God and as proceeding from the Father. The New Testament writers do not fall into the mistake of making him his own father, like some modern theologians. If Christ was derived from God, he cannot be coeval with him.

To show his subordination to God, he constantly represents himself, and is constantly represented by the New Testament writers, as "sent of God," and as doing what he does by and through God: "Now they have known that all things whatsoever *thou hast given me* are of thee" (John xvii. 7). "For I have given unto them the words which *thou gavest me;* and they have received them, and have known surely *that I came out from thee*, and they have believed that thou *didst send me*." Here he represents himself as being sent of God, — an admission of subordination. He also declares that he came out from God; that is, that he was derived from God. These two texts would seem sufficient to disprove the equality of source, power, and being. Surely, if he were the supreme God, why thus express his subordination to a higher power, — for the *sent* must derive his authority from the *Sender?* This idea of Christ, that he was commissioned of God (not God himself), is frequently iterated. "O righteous Father, the world hath not known thee; but I have known thee, and these have known that thou hast sent me" (John xvii. 25). "As the Father gave me commandment, even so I do" (John xiv. 31). "I came forth from the Father, and am come into the world" (John xvi. 28). A still more positive assertion of dependence, since it follows a denial of his independence, is this text, which seems to me to be final on this subject of his being coeval with God: "For I proceeded forth and came from God; neither came I of myself, but he sent me" (John viii. 42).

He seems specially careful to keep this idea before his disciples, who, he feared, like the impulsive Greeks when Paul and Barnabas preached to them, would be too ready to make a god of him. He was therefore careful to recognize God as the author of his life, and with reverence and piety to thank him for the gift. Paul seems to have had the same idea, that Christ's life was the gift of God: "For though he was crucified through weakness, yet he liveth by the power of God" (2 Cor. xiii. 4). Paul goes even farther in this verse, and says that this ineffable and abundant life, which the Father had given to the Son (John v. 26), his disciples may also have from the same source: "For we also are weak in him, but we shall live with him by the power of God toward you."

Closely connected with this express declaration of derivation from God is his constant assertion of his dependence upon God, showing that he owed to God not only the origin of his life, but also its maintenance; that he was dependent upon God for the power by which all his works were done. As expressing this dependence, Jesus says, "Verily, I say unto you, The Son can do *nothing of himself*, but what he seeth the Father do" (John v. 19).

The assertion is repeated in John v. 30, "I can of *mine own self do nothing.*"

In John x. 25, he declares that his works were done in his Father's name.

Recognizing God's authority, Jesus declared himself entirely guided and controlled by his will: "For I came down from heaven, not to do mine own will, but the will of him that sent me" (John vi. 38); "The Father which sent me, he gave me a commandment" (John xii. 49); "Even as the Father said unto me, so I speak" (John xii. 50); "As my Father hath taught me, I speak these things" (John viii. 28).

Akin to his denial of omnipotence is his denial of omniscience: "But of that day and that hour knoweth no man, no, not the angels which are in heaven, neither the Son, but the *Father*" (Mark xiii. 32).

It is with a sense of his own weakness, his despised and rejected condition, that he prays unto his Father to be glorified of him: "Father, glorify thy Son, that thy Son also may glorify thee" (John xvii. 1). Again, "I seek not mine own glory. . . . I honor my Father" (John viii. 49, 50).

How can we suppose, if he were the supreme God, the source, possessor, and dispenser of all glory, that he should pray to another and higher being for that glory which he already possessed? It is really to accuse Christ of prevarication, whatever the intention may be. And the case is not at all relieved of these elements, if it is said that he prayed unto himself; for, as supreme God, he had no need to pray unto himself: it was only a mockery of true prayer. Jesus evidently thought so; for he said, "If I honor myself, my honor is nothing: it is my Father that honoreth me" (John viii. 54).

Jesus not only repeatedly called God his *Father*, and taught his disciples so to call him, but he also calls him his *God:* "Jesus saith unto her, Go to my brethren, and say unto them, I ascend unto my Father and your Father, to my God and your God." Here it is seen that Christ worshipped the same God as his disciples. As he denied the possession of supreme power himself, and referred his power, authority, and existence to God, so we might expect that he would direct his Apostles to recognize and worship God the Father as the great source of being and of power. Priests and ecclesiastical councils have insisted that we should worship Jesus, but with no authority from him. His direction to his disciples was, "When ye pray say, Our Father which art in heaven." He presents us the Father as the true object of worship. "The hour cometh, and now is, when the true worshippers shall worship the Father in spirit and in truth; for the Father seeketh such to worship him."

Establish his derivation and dependence, and his subordination follows as a logical sequence. But he did not leave this to be inferred or reasoned out. He asserted it in the most positive and unambiguous language: "*My Father is greater than I*" (John xiv. 28). If there were no other passage in the New Testament on this subject, this would be conclusive.

CONCLUSIONS STATED.

After such an array of gospel testimony, it would seem that nothing more would be needed to confirm our belief that the obvious and direct teaching of the New Testament declares the existence of God, the Father, the existence of his Son, and the distinctness of each; that, further, Christ existed by and for him; that all his authority and power were given him by the Father, and that he was not and could not be equal with the Father, because he expressly denies the possession of attributes which could belong only to a God, and which we are accustomed to predicate of God,—his omnipotence, omniscience, self-existence, independence, — and even in one place denying that he possesses that pre-eminent goodness which we ascribe to God: "Why callest thou *me* good? There is none good but one, that is God." We cannot suppose that Christ could be the supreme God and yet deny the superiority he possessed. Nor could we suppose, with all confidence in his purity and nobleness of character, his sincerity and transparent ingenuousness, that he would assert himself to be supreme when he was not. Nor does he. He was guiltless of the orthodox creeds. He was too conscious of his own dependence on God to disown the source of his exalted manhood and the seal and credentials of his divinity.

Nor did his immediate disciples, who were charged full of his love and fired by its zeal, pervert the idea that Christ presented of himself. Jesus was made "God," not *in* the Scripture, but *out* of it. It seems impossible to me that one can search the Scriptures upon this point, and deduce from them the absolute supremacy of Christ, without going to the examination with preconceived ideas, which he is determined to establish.

Observe that in making this examination I have not rested my conclusion upon the authority of a single text, but of a great many, sufficient, I think, to show the correct and general direction of Scripture teaching.

Am I to be judged harshly, if I prefer the Scriptures themselves to what somebody says about them, or to conjectures made from them? Am I to be judged, if I prefer to sit out under the clear, God-lit sky of revelation, and take the life-giving, life-warming truth from the great central source itself, rather than to look through the smoked glass of a mediæval interpretation?

About half of this lengthy treatise was devoted to an examination of Scripture passages which are supposed to defend the deity of Jesus. I have no space to copy them here, and it is not necessary. The work has been better done by representative Unitarian writers. The exegetical part of the argument was concluded by quoting a few texts from the Epistles which confirmed the testimony of the Gospels; namely, the words of Paul. "There is one God, and one mediator between God and man, the man Christ Jesus." Again, the subjection of Christ declared in 1 Cor. xv. 27, 28: "But when he saith all things are put under him, it is manifest that he is excepted, which did put all things under him. When all things shall be subdued unto him, then shall the Son also himself be subject unto him that put all things under him, that God may be all in all."

As to the orthodox side of the doctrine, Asked-of-God was familiar with it, not only in a general way from his childhood, but by a special study of orthodox writers when he made this examination. But the Biblical strength of the Unitarian position was a fresh revelation to him, and reason and revelation seemed to be in consonance with it.

But though he could no longer on Scriptural or rational grounds believe in the deity of Jesus, he believed as strongly as ever in the divinity of his mission and the power of his life. His article concluded as follows : —

I do not concern myself with the metaphysics of Christ's nature. It is the least satisfactory way of viewing him. I do not attempt to measure him or limit him by a cold scientific definition. There is a blank in the history which has not yet been filled. But though we do not know all that he was and all that he might have been, had he not been cut off by an early death, we may know enough to be saved by his life, if we will follow his example.

XX.

A SIGNIFICANT LETTER.

IN the two previous chapters I have given some results of Asked-of-God's study of the Bible. He could no longer, on Biblical grounds, accept the doctrine of the Trinity as taught in the churches; nor could he accept the absolute deity of Jesus. There was a third point in which his opinions also suffered a great change, and that was in regard to the atonement. The language of the New Testament was highly figurative. Taken literally, it could easily be used to support current orthodox theories. But Asked-of-God now saw in its metaphor a general expression of the great law of sacrifice, which is illustrated in all human history. He reached the conclusion that the life and death of Jesus were not needed to affect the disposition of God, but to inspire in humanity a love for truth and righteousness.

Though he was mainly influenced in his conclusions by his study of the Bible, he availed himself of such books as seemed to throw light upon its pages. He found help and satisfaction in tracts by the Rev. A. P. Peabody, D.D., the Rev. William G. Eliot, D.D., Dr. Henry W. Bellows, and others, which were kindly furnished to him by a Unitarian friend. "Orthodoxy: its Truths and Errors," by

James Freeman Clarke, was also valued highly for its candor of tone and simplicity of statement.

But it must not be thought that Asked-of-God was living in a Unitarian atmosphere. On the contrary, nearly all his surroundings and associations were opposed to it. He was engaged every Sunday morning in reporting the sermon of the leading Methodist preacher in Washington at that time. He was recording secretary of the Young Men's Christian Association, and was a teacher and officer in a large colored mission school, mainly conducted by members of the Congregational (Trinitarian) Church. He also attended, during the two winters he was most actively engaged in these investigations, the Theological School connected with Columbian College. The school was administered and controlled entirely by Baptists. The leading man in the Faculty was the Greek professor, the Rev. Dr. Huntington, of whose learning, candor, and kindness the student has still a grateful and appreciative remembrance.

Thus it will be seen that attending a Methodist church Sunday morning, an Orthodox Sunday-school in the afternoon, and a Baptist Theological Seminary during the week, he was not unduly biased by Unitarian influence. He had developed considerable individuality, however, in his opinions. One Sunday afternoon, while making a round of calls in a colored district to secure more children for the Sunday-school, he found a colored woman who was a Catholic, while her husband was a Methodist. The woman stated that she and her husband got on very well together. "Every tub," she said, "must stand on its own bottom." Asked-of-God himself had come to this conclusion.

The small and unattractive Unitarian church on Sixth Street had not escaped his notice. Being engaged every Sunday morning catching the droppings of the Methodist pulpit, his visits to the Unitarian church, like those of Nicodemus in his search for truth, had to be made at night. The pulpit was supplied at this period by an elderly gentleman of commanding appearance and a magnificent bass voice, which rolled out Unitarian affirmations with unmistakable emphasis and power. A course of doctrinal sermons on Unitarian views of God, Christ, and the Bible were listened to, as opportunity afforded, with great satisfaction; and Asked-of-God is only too glad to render testimony to the efficient and earnest ministry of the late Dr. Rufus P. Stebbins. Occasionally Dr. Bellows came to the capital; and an acquaintance formed with him at this time proved to be of great value and help to the student.

It was quite evident that Asked-of-God was nearing a new epoch in his life.

And now what of the old Baptist church, from whose fellowship and service he had been geographically separated for several years? Had they forgotten their absent sheep? The pastor who baptized him had removed to another field. The church itself in New York had removed to a different part of the city, but the name of the young convert was still on its books. Rich and delightful were the associations connected with the old meeting-house and its members. Asked-of-God did not wish to take the first step to sever them, nor did he have to.

The subject of his church relations was assuming a new importance to him, when, one day, the mail brought a significant document. It was in the form of a circular letter from the church in New York of which he was a member. It stated that, on reviewing the church list, the name of Asked-of-God was found upon it; and, not having heard from him for a long time, this method was adopted to ascertain his religious condition. Satisfactory answers were asked to several questions whose consideration, it was hoped, would be profitable to the recipient. The questions were: —

1. Are you living in the habitual performance of Christian duty and the enjoyment of the Saviour's presence?

2. Is there a Baptist church in your vicinity? If so, what is the pastor's name and address?

3. Is it possible for you to attend worship with them, and do you attend regularly?

4. Are you permanently settled in your present place of residence?

5. Ought you not to take your letter and unite with the church in which you worship?

6. Should you not contribute *something* to the church of which you are a member and where your name stands?

The letter concluded as follows: —

We hope that, as in the presence of the Great Searcher of Hearts, you will prayerfully consider the above inquiries, and transmit to us your reply as soon as possible. And be assured, dear brother, that we feel a deep interest in your temporal and eternal welfare, and have adopted this as the best course of fulfilling our covenant engagements with you. Praying that the Great Head of the Church will guide and bless you wherever your lot may be cast, we subscribe ourselves your brethren in the Lord.

The letter was signed by the pastor. It came at a time when Asked-of-God was prepared to answer it. He at first wrote a somewhat polemical reply, which he promptly put into the waste-basket, and then prepared another, recognizing the courtesy and kindness of his brethren in the spirit of Christian love which was expressed in their inquiries. He answered the first question in regard to his "habitual performance of Christian duty" by saying that if attending church on Sunday, teaching in a mission school, and working with the Young Men's Christian Association as its secretary were to be considered Christian duties, he might say that he was living in the habitual performance of them; but if Christian duty comprehended all our duties to God and man, whether inside of a church or outside of it, then he felt that he could not say that he lived up to his ideal. In regard to the "enjoyment of his Saviour's presence," he gave an outline of the new relation in which Jesus appeared to him and the inspiration derived from his example. Though his thought of Jesus had changed, admiration and love for his character had only increased.

In reply to the fifth question, "Ought you not to take your letter and unite with the church with which you worship?" he answered, with a slight sense of humor, that he was a regular worshipper at the Methodist church, and inquired whether his Baptist brethren would be kind enough to give him a letter of dismission to that church. He did not state that he was paid a stipulated sum for his attendance and services.

Asked-of-God did not fail to indicate very frankly the new conclusions he had reached. He waited with much interest to see what penalty he must pay for them.

XXI.

LABORING WITH A HERETIC.

ASKED-OF-GOD had unbosomed his convictions to his mother church. He had answered the letter sent to him with distinctness and without ambiguity. And now what did the brethren think of it?

The Baptists claim to derive the principles of their discipline from the New Testament. It is not a part of their method, therefore, to exclude one of their members without first generously laboring for his restoration. The attitude of the church and its pastor on discovering the heresy of their wayward member will be seen from the following letter, which they sent to him a few weeks later. I have preserved the italics with which it was emphasized.

To ASKED-OF-GOD, Washington, D.C. :

MY DEAR BROTHER, — We received your letter, dated in April, and presented it to the church at the church meeting held May 1. The brethren generally, and especially your personal acquaintances, were very much surprised and grieved at its contents. The church desires your best welfare, and requests me to write to you before proceeding to any further action in the case. The pressure of other duties has prevented me until now from undertaking this; and now, I fear, it will have to be very imperfectly performed.

I enter upon this work with no dependence upon my own logical powers to effect any good result; but if it shall please our dear Heavenly Father to bless what I may write to your conversion (James v. 19), I shall be grateful to him and give him all the praise.

I am not at all surprised that in these "last, perilous times" *many* professed Christians are led away by the specious errors which so abound, even though some of these errors, under the name of Christianity, deny Christianity's central truth, the atoning work of Christ. For this is clearly predicted in the Inspired Word; and the very system with which you have unfortunately identified yourself is described in unmistakable language by the Apostle Peter in his Second Epistle (chap. ii. 1, 2).

The difference between us is *not* "one of interpretation" merely. I claim that we receive *all* the teaching of God's Word, while Unitarianism receives only *a part* and *denies a part;* and the part it denies is the *essential* part to man's salvation. For while orthodox Christians lay no less stress than Unitarians on the moral requirements of the law and the gospel, including, of course, the grand summary of the law, "Thou shalt love the Lord thy God with all thy heart, and thy neighbor as thyself," they also accept those declarations which teach that "by the deeds of the law shall no flesh be justified in his sight," holding with Paul that "after that the kindness and love of *God our Saviour* toward man appeared, *not* by *works of righteousness* which *we* have done, but *according to his mercy* he saved us, by the washing of regeneration and *renewing* of the *Holy Ghost*, which he shed on us abundantly through Jesus Christ our Saviour; that, being *justified by his grace*, we should *be made heirs* according to the hope of eternal life. This is a faithful saying; and these things I will that thou affirm constantly, that *they which have believed in God* might be careful to *maintain good* works" (Titus iii. 4–8).

You speak, in your letter, of Christ living and dying to save us, and then add, "or, as *he more pointedly states the object of his life*, that he came to bear witness to the truth." Can you tell me, my dear brother, *where* Jesus *ever* said that? *I* can tell *you* where he said that "he came to seek and *to save* that which was lost" (Luke xix. 10; Matt. xviii. 11), "to *give his life a ransom* for many" (Matt. xx. 28; Mark x. 45), "to *lay down his life* for the sheep" (John x. 11, 15,.17, 18). And I can point you to numerous declarations of the inspired apostles, attesting the same truth in the most unequivocal language, the following among others: "Christ hath *redeemed* us from the curse of the law, being *made a curse for us*" (Gal. iii. 13); "Forasmuch as ye know that ye were . . . *redeemed* . . . with the *precious blood of Christ*, as of a lamb without blemish and without spot" (1 Peter i. 18, 19); "Thou wast slain, and hast *redeemed* us to God *by thy blood*" (Rev. v. 9); "Christ died for our sins" (1 Cor. xv. 3); "Christ *died for the ungodly*," "While we were yet sinners, *Christ died for us*" (Rom. v. 6, 8); "Our Lord Jesus Christ *died for* us" (1 Thess. v. 10); "Our Saviour Jesus Christ, who *gave himself for us*, that he might *redeem* us from all iniquity, and *purify* unto himself a peculiar people, zealous of good works" (Titus ii. 13, 14). But I *never* find Christ or the Apostles speaking of Jesus as a witness (μάρτυρ).

And it seems to me that this fact indicates the foreknowledge of Jesus and the Holy Spirit of the coming of that system of error which should seek to degrade Christ from the office of an atoning Saviour to a mere witness or martyr.

The letter then passed to consider the Godhead of Jesus, and quoted John x. 30; xiv. 9, 11; Acts x. 25, 26; xiv. 13, 15; Revelation xxii. 8, 9; John i. 1, 14; Romans ix. 5; Titus ii. 13. After marshalling these texts, the letter continued:—

The *humanity* of Jesus is very precious to us as assuring us of his sympathy and affording us a perfect example; but his *divinity* is *more* precious, as affording the assurance that he is "mighty to save." "Great is the mystery of godliness: God was manifest in the flesh" (1 Tim. iii. 16). And here permit me to say that a divine Revelation must have mysteries to us, unless we also possess divine powers; for a Revelation which human reason can fathom we may logically conclude is the product of a human mind. But a Revelation beyond, though not inconsistent with human reason, bears intrinsic evidence of its superhuman origin. The gospel is not for philosophers only, but for all who as "little children" will receive it. From the "wise and prudent" in worldly philosophy these things must be "hidden," after all their "investigations;" but to the "babes" God "reveals" the mysteries of his kingdom (Matt. xi. 25, 26).

The "Age of Reason" must ever be an age of infidelity in reference to divine truths; for human reason is too proud to confess its own inability to discover truth. "The world by wisdom knew not God," and never will. Search, my dear brother, the Word of God through, and you will never find any inspired writer ever claiming to have "discovered" any spiritual truth by his own "investigations," but constantly honoring God as the source of his knowledge, — God having "revealed" the truth unto him by his Spirit. 1 Cor. i. 27–29 and ii. 1–16 are in point here. Read them humbly, and see whether I do not harmonize with the divine teaching more than those who exalt Reason as the umpire of Revelation.

There are some portions of your letter that are shocking to your brethren; and I can only kindly and faithfully admonish you that you are making shipwreck of the faith which alone can justify and save a sinner, — faith in the atoning blood of Jesus. "For even Christ *our passover* is *sacrificed for us*" (1 Cor. v. 7), and "without [the] shedding of [his] blood there is no remission" (Heb. ix. 22, 28). I think I discover (what perhaps you are scarcely conscious of) that pride of intellect is at the bottom of your rejection of the fundamental truths of the Gospels, forgetting the admonition of the wise man, "Trust in the Lord with all thine heart, *and lean not to thine own understanding*" (Prov. iii. 5). In all your letter, you have quoted but two texts from the Word of God, and have given as the words of Jesus what he never uttered.

Now, we act on this teaching of Jesus, and to all those who "hold the Head" we extend fellowship. But we *cannot* fellowship those who set up a rival to the Head. And when persons undertake to cast out devils *in some other name*, while we do not interfere with their civil or religious liberty, we simply bear our testimony to the world that they are "not for us, but against us."

These things speak little in favor of your biblical knowledge or your disposition to be governed by God's revealed will, and what you hold to be the truth is rather the deductions of reason than the reception of Revelation. I earnestly beseech you to read prayerfully and carefully the first chapter of Paul's Epistle to the Romans, and there you will learn the sure gradations of unbelief. Need I tell you that social evils of the most vile and alarming character are already the outgrowth of Unitarianism, — "Liberal Christianity," as it terms itself? I pray you pause, my brother, before you finally commit yourself to a system which "denies the Lord that bought you," and strives to substitute in his place a creature who merely sets you a good example, — an example, however, so pure and holy that none but the incarnate God could have set it, and nothing but the power of a Divine Saviour received by simple faith can enable us even imperfectly to imitate it.

Asking to hear from you again, and praying that God may bless these imperfect lines to your salvation from grievous and dangerous error, I remain.

       YOUR AFFECTIONATE PASTOR.

I will not attempt to describe the emotions with which Asked-of-God received this letter. I am sure they will best be seen in the answer which he prepared to it, and which was duly submitted to the church. Covering as it does some forty-eight pages of foolscap, I am somewhat in doubt whether Asked-of-God, who prepared this reply, was more entitled to sympathy or the brethren who were forced to read it. But the student was dead in earnest.

WASHINGTON CITY.

MY DEAR BROTHER,—Yours of June 28 came duly to hand. I thank the church for the forbearance with which it has treated my case, — that it has preferred to make some effort to reclaim one whom it deems an erring brother rather than hastily and harshly to erase his name from its books. I appreciate your fidelity in fulfilling the request of the church in discharging what seems to have been a duty rather than a pleasure. Had your impulse been any motive weaker than a duty, I could readily see how you could have left from your letter some things which detracted from the general agreeableness and charity of its tone. I attribute it to no unkindness of feeling, but rather to the natural tendency of the Calvinistic view, that you feel it your duty to class me with "false teachers and prophets who have brought in damnable heresies, even denying the Lord that bought them and bringing upon themselves swift destruction," "whose judgment now of long time lingereth not and whose damnation slumbereth not." The association, I must confess, does not seem pleasant. Nor is it any pleasanter to turn to the first chapter of Romans and read there "the sure gradations of unbelief" through which I am expected to pass, — to feel that God has given me over "to a reprobate mind, to do those things which are not convenient; being filled with all unrighteousness, fornication, wickedness, covetousness, maliciousness; full of envy, murder, debate, deceit, malignity; whisperers, ... haters of God," etc.

I can only fervently hope, dear brother, that in this estimate of my danger you may be mistaken. I have ground for the hope that you may be mistaken, in the fact that the great leading light of Unitarianism, William Ellery Channing, though according to your belief a heretic, was not in any respect what is there described by Paul, but rather that he was "pure, peaceable, gentle, easy to be entreated, full of mercy and good fruits, without partiality and without hypocrisy" (James iii. 17). When I look at the characters of Ware, Martineau, Bellows, Collyer, Hedge, and Clarke, I can see nothing that warrants an application to them of these words of Paul.

Another passage of Paul's came to my mind as I read that portion of your letter. It is found in the fourteenth chapter of Romans, and reads, "Who art thou that judgest another man's servant? to his own master he standeth or falleth." And in the tenth verse: "Why dost thou set at nought thy brother? we shall all stand before the judgment seat of Christ." "Let us not therefore judge one another any more: but judge this rather, that no man put a stumbling-block or an occasion to fall in his brother's way."

I think it is always dangerous, brother, to quote against another the first chapter of Romans, or indeed any other chapter, unless you have studied well the fourteenth.

I cannot count it as a slip of the pen, but only as a singular want of knowledge, which made you say that "social evils of the most vile and alarming character are the outgrowth of Unitarianism." You did not point to any single one, but contented yourself with levelling against the denomination a general charge, which has no foundation in fact, and which honest investigation would show you to be untrue. On the contrary, Unitarianism is no more distinguished for its high culture and refinement and intellectual strength than for the earnest piety and philanthropy it has cultivated and developed. And if you can gauge the faith, spirituality, and righteousness of the Unitarian denomination, I sincerely believe that in these respects no comparison with any denomination you could make would be to its disadvantage.

I hasten, then, in the beginning to deny these aspersions, because a prompt and emphatic denial of them is the only just treatment they can receive. In such a matter argument is out of the question: we must resort to facts. Immorality wearing simply the Unitarian name is no more chargeable upon true Unitarianism than is the waywardness of any particular one of your members chargeable to the religious views of your denomination. One morning last fall, in New York, I learned that the man with whom I had been baptized, on entering your church, had been arrested for drunkenness the night before, and lodged in the station-house. He is a Baptist; but would it be fair for me to cite him as an illustration of the tendency of Baptist views, as a fair sample of the denomination? Would it be fair, either, for critics of your denomination to say that, because the writer of this letter has felt at liberty to think for himself, all Baptists take the same liberty? By no means: I should be one of the first to deny the charge. And so, where you find an exceptional "Unitarian," so called, leading a life that is not true, is it any fairer to charge his obliquities upon the whole denomination? Is not the true way to see what are the average morality and character of the denomination before making a criticism which, though true of individuals, may be a great libel upon the majority? However *you* may view it, my own regard for character is such that I am no more willing to have those with whom I associate stigmatized than I am to be stigmatized myself.

And, brother, let me suggest to you as a Baptist minister — who, in view of the rapid and determined progress of free thought, may feel it necessary in the course of your ministry to write more than one such letter to the erring — that the most unsuccessful way to convert a sinner from the error of his ways is to say things of him or his principles that are neither courteous nor true.

Take in all kindness this criticism, and now let me refer you to the argument.

Asked-of-God took up the Scripture argument in detail. He expressed his willingness to accept the testimony of Jesus, saying, —

I believe it to be my privilege to interpret the words of Christ in accordance with reason, morality, the principles of justice, and the law of infinite love. I am willing to obey Christ, but not all of his interpreters. I know it may be difficult for you to understand how I can study the Bible sincerely and yet come to any other conclusions than yours about his teachings. But you will scarcely claim infallibility; and if such a study by me establishes my present convictions, please tell me what is left for me to do but to obey them. . . .

My own belief, and the Unitarian belief generally, is as positive as your own. We believe in the verities of Godhead and manhood and immortality as strongly as you. We believe in Christ, we believe in God, we believe in future reward and in future punishment; and we find all of these taught in the Bible.

Asked-of-God then reviewed all the texts his pastor had quoted, and showed how easily they could be interpreted in conformity with Unitarian doctrine. The unsatisfactoriness of all argument founded merely on exegetical study was shown in this discussion. Many texts furnish as good weapons for one side as for the other, when taken singly. They are like arrows which will go in any direction in which they are sent.

After giving his array of Scripture truths in regard to the nature and work of Christ, Asked-of-God wrote: —

We differ in this. You believe that Christ came here mainly to die. I believe that he came here mainly to live; his death being an important incident in the record of his history, and calculated from the circumstances that attended it to draw men to the contemplation of that blameless life of whose perfection and obedience it was the glorious culmination. You feel it necessary to believe that Christ came here to deliver us from the *arbitrary wrath of God*, — not merely from the natural penalties of sin which God has attached to the violations of his law, but to save us from an everlasting pit which he has in store for all those who have inherited the guilt and transgression of Adam, — and by offering up himself and his blood to that Father to appease his outraged justice, and so *buy* that salvation for men which they would never obtain from God's mercy alone. I prefer, on the other hand, to believe that Christ came into this world to "save sinners" (from their transgression), that he came "to seek and to save that which was lost," "to quicken those who are dead in trespasses and sin," and by the power of his life awaken them *to righteousness.* I prefer to believe that Christ is the *way*, the *truth*, and the *life;* that he was the *way* by which we come into clearer conceptions of truth and life, — the way by which, if we walk therein, we shall be saved from sin and attain to the glorious inheritance of the saints in light. I believe that he is the *truth;* and that if we believe in that truth, the truth shall make us free, — free from the power of sin within, and free from the power of sin without, the soul. I believe that he is the *life:* if we live in him we shall have "life more abundantly," — our life shall be expanded in its capacities, in its joys, its privileges, and its fruits; that the man who is out of Christ only half lives, but he that is in Christ has that "eternal life" which comes from knowing the only true God and Jesus Christ whom he has sent.

Asked-of-God did not fail to express his astonishment that Jesus' words to Pilate, " To this end was I born, and for this cause came I into the world, that I should bear witness unto the truth," had made little or no impression upon his pastor's memory. When, therefore, he was asked for evidence that Jesus was a witness (martyr) to the truth, it was with much satisfaction that he referred to this passage (John xviii. 18). "If," he added, "it is a system of error to believe in Christ as bearing witness to the truth, then Christ was the founder of that system; for he declared that to be his purpose."

In closing his letter, Asked-of-God said: —

Dear brother, I have said more than I intended; perhaps not more than was needed. Accept in all kindness what I have written; attribute to earnestness and warmth of argument any overheat of tone the letter may display, and express to my brethren there my cordial thanks for their moderation and the best wishes for their continued prosperity and usefulness. We are journeying toward a common goal, battling for a common purpose: let us not be too critical of our minor beliefs and inferior speculations; but when we come to determine the cardinal entities of life as declared in Christianity, let us remember that no other foundation can man lay than that which is laid, which is Jesus Christ. That foundation is the foundation of *truth;* no other will last. Tell my brethren I have not given up the idea of greeting them in that happy yonder land; that I do not expect to go in as a thief and robber, but to go through the *door* and the *way* which God has provided for his children to come home to their Father's mansion, — his infinite and ever-pardoning love, of which Christ was the unspeakable gift.

It will be seen from the preceding pages that the discussion which Asked-of-God held with his Baptist friends in regard to his change of views was conducted largely with reference to the Bible as the chief source of appeal. It was natural that this should be so; because, first, the Bible was to Baptists the infallible source of authority in all religious matters; and, secondly, because it was largely through an earnest and candid study of its contents that Asked-of-God had been led to revise his beliefs concerning the central doctrines of Christianity. I am still disposed to maintain that the views which he reached from Bible study much more closely resembled those held by the primitive Christian Church than the formal set of doctrines which are commonly said to be "evangelical," especially those bearing the stamp of Calvinism. Later, however, he saw that it was necessary to subject to a rigid examination the claim made for the Bible as an infallible revelation. He then found that the Bible was a collection of many books, written by many different hands in a period extending over several centuries. Instead of being supernaturally dictated by God, its various books were written under natural human conditions, and exhibited the errors and imperfections as well as the inspiration possible to fallible humanity. These books had been collected not by any revelation from God, but through the fallible though generally wise sentiment of the Christian

Church as to their merits. The autograph manuscripts of the books were long since destroyed. The original text could not be completely recovered.

It was therefore impossible, both from external and internal considerations, to regard the Bible as an infallible book. While many of its pages still glowed with the inspiration of its writers, others contained views of God and of duty which could no longer be accepted as binding upon the reason and conscience of mankind. They were interesting and valuable as a part of the record of the religious history of the race; but these milestones of history were not to be piled up as barriers across the pathway of human progress. In short, the Bible itself, instead of being the sole arbiter of truth, was simply a part of the sacred literature of the world, and was itself to be tested by the reason and the enlightened moral judgments of mankind. This view of the Bible did not diminish in any degree its essential merits; and whatever truth it contained had the authority which all truth possesses.

The Roman Catholic church holds with great tenacity to its dogma of an infallible Pope, and the Protestant church has held with equal tenacity to its infallible Bible. It has been assumed that there is no safe foundation for an organized church unless its religious tenets rest upon an infallibility of some sort. The history of Protestantism shows that it is of little use to claim absolute authority for a book without an inflexible interpretation. It has been easy to read into the Bible a meaning which it has seemed desirable or necessary to get out of it. Hence each sect has claimed it as its own. But Asked-of-God now came to feel that the pursuit of truth, free from all trammels, was in itself far more inspiring and invigorating than reliance upon any traditional or ecclesiastical authority. Absolute certainty was not to be expected; complete knowledge was not possible; but entire freedom in the search for truth was essential to the attainment of that measure of knowledge and certitude which is possible to humanity. The claim of infallibility in church, pope, or Bible was not only seen to be fictitious, but also unnecessary. Absolute knowledge is no more essential to the safety of the Church than to the safety of the home or the State. Our knowledge shades off into half-knowledge, and our half-knowledge into the dim twilight of uncertainty. It is the function of the Church to furnish a working rule of life rather than one which is incapable of expansion or change. The larger word of God is not bound. There is more light to break forth from its unnumbered pages; and, day by day and year by year, the prediction of Jesus is being fulfilled: "Ye shall know the truth, and the truth shall make you free."

XXII.

EXCOMMUNICATED.

ONE of the most agreeable ways of conducting an ecclesiastical trial is to conduct it through the mail. Undoubtedly many of the ancient heretics would have preferred to be arraigned at a distance of two hundred and fifty miles from their persecutors. This was about the distance that separated Asked-of-God from the old Baptist meeting-house. I would not undertake to measure in miles the extent of his theological deviation. No odometer has yet been invented to record the distance which heretics may wander from the fold. Though obliged by this distance from the old church to communicate his views entirely by mail, he would gladly have exchanged his pen for an opportunity to plead his own cause before his brethren face to face. But the opportunity did not come. His official correspondence with the church closed with the letter published in the last chapter. He received, however, an anonymous letter, of much the same tenor as the letter from his pastor, from an earnest and anxious member, laboring, by Scripture arguments and strong personal appeal, to reconvert him. It would have been as easy for the brother to take a vigorous sapling and put it back into the seed again, or to put a chicken back into the egg, as to put the young convert back into the limitations of his old faith.

In due time he learned that the church had dropped him from its roll of membership: he was excommunicated. Vastly different is the signification of this word to-day than when indited a few centuries since, loaded with all the terrors of Roman Catholic rigor. It brought with it no penalties but the severing of old and much-loved ties. Let the noble services which the Baptist church in the early years of its history rendered to the cause of civil and religious liberty be fully recognized. That church gave up all claim to persecute its wayward members through the civil power; and, fortunately, civil liberty has made such progress that no other church can avail itself of the old method of roasting its heretics. The Baptists, in the matter of discipline, profess to follow strictly the New Testament rule. To their credit, let it be said that they did so in this case. They had labored to reclaim an erring brother. Their efforts had proved unavailing. There was but one course left to them, according to the usage of their church. It was to drop him from its rolls. Yet I am sure this final action was not taken without some prayer for his reclamation.

Separated geographically as he was from his brethren, the fact of his excommunication made no practical difference in his personal relations to members of the old church. His name had simply been crossed from the church rolls. And yet it was something more than a mere clerical matter. He did not view it with indifference.

It was a turning-point in his life. It brought back vividly the history of his past. Tender and sacred associations crowded into his memory. Once more there came up before his mind a picture of the infant class, in which a saintly teacher had tried to teach him the way to God. There was the image of the faithful man who, later on, had succeeded to her office. Loved and familiar faces clustered around them both. It was hard to feel that there must be any gulf between them and him. Then came up the picture of the memorable night when he timidly made his way up the staircase into the inquiry-room, and then the still more vivid picture of the evening when he descended into the baptismal waters. How intense had been the joy of his heart when he had joined that band of disciples and started with them on the journey to heaven; for that was the goal that was constantly kept before the mind! These loved pictures still hung in the gallery of his memory: he could not turn their faces to the wall. The thought of mental and spiritual exile from this early habitation of his mind and heart was extremely painful.

There was another aspect in which this change was still more painful. He knew that it would bring deep sorrow to those united to him by ties of blood and by still more enduring ties of affection. Gladly would he have done anything which his convictions permitted to avert the deep pain which came to the mother that bore him. There are no conflicts so painful as those when the conscience and the intellect come into collision with the affections; and yet how can they be averted? When the parent bird has taught its little ones to fly for themselves, it has taken the first step toward finally separating them from the nest in which they were reared. The only way to have kept Asked-of-God in the old Baptist nest would have been to pinion his wings.

It would have mitigated the pain of his separation if his friends could have regarded it as one of those separations which come from growth. To many of them, however, it seemed the result of spiritual declension and obduracy of heart. Asked-of-God knew that to those of his old friends who held logically to their system of belief, his excommunication from the church had a deeper significance than simply an estrangement of earthly ties. It meant that they saw no reason to feel that he was any longer a child of God; that they could no longer feel that his conversion was genuine, and that the blood of Jesus had been applied to wash away his sins; in short, they could entertain no hope that the heaven to which they looked forward was to be his eternal home. To some who had been his moral and spiritual guardians, this thought must have brought deep distress, as it had brought pain to the heart of Asked-of-God when he had held such views himself. His brethren of the old meeting-house knew nothing of that gentle ministry of sunshine, dew, and shower under which his soul had expanded into new growth. They saw not the process: they saw only the result. He had been a Baptist: he had now become theologically and spiritually an outcast. To most of them it was unaccountable. But there was one stern and rigid

Calvinist in the old meeting-house, who, with all his goodness of heart, was mercilessly consistent. He could find in Paul's letter to the Thessalonians a temporary explanation. "God shall send them strong delusion, that they should believe a lie: that they all might be damned who believed not the truth, but had pleasure in unrighteousness" (2 Thess. ii. 11). I say, a temporary explanation; for while the Calvinist might believe that God had turned over a member of the visible church to a reprobate mind, he had also another avenue for the exercise of hope and faith in his reformation. Believing as the Baptists do in the perseverance of the saints, there were those who still cherished the hope that Asked-of-God was only suffering a temporary aberration, and that by and by he would be restored to the fold; and unless their affection for him has decreased more than I am willing to believe, such prayers are still offered on his behalf.

But if his excommunication from the old church brought with it unavoidable sadness, it also awakened feelings of indescribable gladness. That the old tie was severed was painful, but the manacles to faith and freedom had gone with it. Once before in his life, he had felt like Christian when he rolled off his burden at the wicket gate. Now he felt in some such way again. He had rolled off the burden of the old theology. A heavy burden it had been to bear. He had put aside a narrow traditional view of the universe; he had abandoned views which were dishonoring to God, which impugned his justice, mercy, and love. He had got rid of traditional views of humanity equally unsatisfactory; but there had come in their place a broad and expansive view of the universe, a lofty conception of God's government, a new hope for the destiny of humanity. If, like Paul, he felt pained to give up the Hebraism in which he had been reared, if his heart went out to his brethren and kinsmen according to the flesh, he rejoiced with joy unspeakable and full of glory in the light that had flooded his way and the voice that had spoken to his heart.

The staircase to the inquiry-room, by which twelve years before he had entered the Baptist meeting-house, was steep and narrow. It was for him the staircase to the old faith. But now that he left the much-loved church, it was through the broad aisle and the open door. It led to a new faith and a larger fellowship. His excommunication revealed the Apocalyptic message, "*I have set before thee an open door, and no man can shut it.*"

XXIII.

SEEKING A HOME.

ASKED-OF-GOD had been shut out from the Baptist fold. Ecclesiastically, he was homeless; but he did not intend to remain so. He was not content with the individualism of Diogenes to live in a tub alone by himself. Association was a necessity of his nature. Where should he find it? He already enjoyed it to a considerable extent in his active and practical relations with fellow-laborers in benevolent and religious work, but this did not fully satisfy him. He wished to be in close and vital relationship with some Christian church. But what Christian church would admit him? Having been reared a Baptist and accustomed to the congregational form of church polity, his convictions on this subject had remained unchanged. Though he attended a Methodist church for two years as a stenographer, he was not ready to accept its form of church government. He had not that fond and intimate association with a liturgy which draws so many liberal-minded people toward the Episcopal church. He most naturally turned, therefore, toward some branch of the Congregational church. Nearly all the intimate and valued friendships he had formed were with members of the Orthodox Congregational society. From a social point, if he found a home in any church he would most naturally find it there. He was urged by influential friends in this society to accept its creed and join its fellowship. It was said that he might put his own private interpretation upon the creed; that it was to be reasonably elastic, and must not be interpreted too literally. But to Asked-of-God there was another question. It was, Could this creed possibly mean the same to him as it did to the rest of those who held it, and as it did to those who made it? He determined to have a conference with the pastor of the Congregational church.

I do not think that Orthodoxy has ever had a better representative in Washington than it had at this time, — a faithful, earnest minister of refined and scholarly tastes, a thorough gentleman in his deportment, and untiring in his devotion to all who had even the slightest claim upon his ministerial offices. His preaching was of the more modern type with reference to its literary methods, but the theology which lay beneath was of the old school. He readily granted the interview which Asked-of-God sought. Together, they considered the question of the Trinity. Perhaps here it might have been possible to patch up an agreement upon some verbal basis. The subject of the divinity of Christ created more difficulty. When they came to the question of the atonement, the gap could not be bridged. With characteristic honesty, the pastor confessed that the inquirer's views were not adequate to admit him to membership in the Orthodox Congregational church. In this conclusion the inquirer entirely agreed. I need hardly say that he had more respect for the pastor than if that gentleman had sought to secure him for the church rolls by weakening his conscience instead of changing his convictions. Much as he enjoyed the society and friendship of many members of that church, Asked-of-God thought that when the two came into conflict, fealty to truth was of more importance than fealty to persons.

There was still another aspect of the case that was influential. New light had come to his soul. He felt that he could not hide it under a bushel. He must let it shine before men. He did not wish to belong to any church in which his views must be concealed or trimmed down to suit any form of creed. He wished to give them large and free expression. Like the woman who had seen and talked with Jesus, he burned to tell others of the new joy he had experienced.

In this state of mind he sought the Unitarian minister, with whom he had frequent conferences. The minister was open-eyed and broad-minded, one who thought more of "religious thinking," as he expressed it, than of "religious thought." The inquirer was not asked to subscribe to any definite statement of thought, but was simply to keep his mind open toward the truth. These conferences were in every way helpful to Asked-of-God, and it was not long before he and his wife and sister-in-law had decided to join the Unitarian church.

This decision occasioned an important change in the fellowship he sustained with other Christian workers. I have stated that he was an active member of the Young

Men's Christian Association, and its recording secretary. The members of that organization are divided into active and associate members. Active members are required to be members of some evangelical church. Associate members become such simply by the payment of the regular annual fee. The active members have the whole control of the organization. Associate members are allowed no voice in its affairs, and furnish rather the material upon which the organization operates. No Unitarian is eligible to active membership in this organization. When, therefore, Asked-of-God determined to join the Unitarian church, he found himself in a peculiar position. He was inside of the Young Men's Christian Association, and would have been glad on many accounts to continue his work with that body. But he could not reconcile it with his conscience to conceal the fact that he had forfeited his membership in the Baptist church, and that he intended to join the Unitarian body. Accordingly, at a regular business meeting of the Association one evening, he rose at the secretary's desk, and stated that he was about to take an important step, which would seriously affect his relations to the Association. He gave a brief outline of the change of views he had experienced. He announced his intention of joining the Unitarian church. He did not seek exclusion or withdrawal from the Association. The ties he had there formed, were dear to him. Though he could no longer agree with his brethren in regard to doctrine, he believed most thoroughly in the practical moral and religious influence which the Association was exerting. But its rules admitted no Unitarian to membership: he could not therefore ask them to extend to him any indulgence which could not be extended to others who shared his convictions. He did not wish to embarrass his brethren by compelling them to take a step which he knew would be painful to them, — that of excluding him from membership. He would therefore relieve them of any such difficulty by offering his resignation as secretary and also as an active member.

No sooner had he taken his seat than the president of the Association, a Major-General in the United States army, jumped to his feet and moved that Asked-of-God be allowed to resign his position as secretary on the ground that he was already overworked, but that his resignation as an active member of the Association be not accepted. While the discussion was pending, Asked-of-God, from a feeling of delicacy, left the room. It was then that one of the venerable pillars of the Association, a strong Calvinistic Presbyterian, arose, and said that the case was perfectly clear. Though regretting the necessity of their secretary's departure, the duty of the Association was evident in the matter. It had taken its doctrinal stand, and could not do otherwise than accept his resignation as an active member.

The heretic had many warm friends in the Association; and it is just possible that, had a vote been taken immediately, the rules might have been relaxed in his favor. The question did not come to a fair issue, however; for one member, seeing a technical loophole of escape, made the point that the secretary had not yet joined the Unitarian Church, and had not received official notification of his exclusion from the Baptist church of which he had been a member. Upon this technical ground, the matter was postponed. Some months later, when Asked-of-God left Washington as a place of permanent residence, his name was quietly dropped from the rolls.

The Methodist minister whose church at Washington he had attended for two years, whose sermons he had constantly reported, with whom he had journeyed across the continent, and whose words he had caught when he stood boldly before ten thousand people in the great tabernacle at Salt Lake and denounced Mormonism to the Mormons,— this Methodist pastor took the announcement of his stenographer's intention to join the Unitarian church without any great manifestation of pain. "Well," he said, "if you have sat under my preaching for two years, and are still going to join the Unitarian church, it is not worth while for me to say anything. I think I have cleared my skirts of your blood." In justice to him, let it be said that he was in no way responsible for his stenographer's change of convictions.

But there were friends who received the announcement that Asked-of-God was to join the Unitarian Church with even more pain than they had learned of his excommunication from the Baptist fold. He has still in his possession a few letters, one of them from a much-loved and much-loving aunt, recording the cry of anguish which went up from her soul when she received this news.

Oh, dear A., when I think of the possibility of your really accepting the Unitarian doctrine as your belief, and my beloved B. and E. doing the same, I cannot be silent in my anguish.

Oh, my child, how can I express to you the *depth* of my grief! To me it looks as if you were turning away from the only door of hope that is opened to us. And what can come of it? To join your communion, I would have to *forfeit* my *only* hope of heaven. If it were held to my choice to join your Unitarian church or perish on the scaffold or in flames, God helping me, how soon would I choose to give up my poor body, that my soul might live! To join the Unitarian church, to *me* would be to turn traitor to my Saviour, to rob him of his divinity, pour contempt on his blood, and, instead of trusting in his righteousness and sacrifice, trying to present the filthy rags of my own righteousness to the sight of a holy God, as cause for my acceptance with him.

And again : —

I look on the Unitarian doctrines as very bad and most dangerous. I have not gone over them, — it does not seem necessary at present; but I would beseech you, as you value the favor of God and a home in *heaven*, *do not* settle down in your new opinions, and think you are all right, for, as sure as the Bible is God's Word, these opinions are wrong.

Such words as these deeply touched the hearts of the new convert and his wife, but they did not change in any way their convictions. It was no longer a question with them of their own personal safety. Asked-of-God and his wife had passed the point when they thought it was possible for a just and holy God to commit his creatures to everlasting torture simply for joining a Unitarian church.

XXIV.

THE NEW HOME AND THE NEW FAITH.

IT was one element of joy in the experience of the jailer who was converted through the instrumentality of Paul and Silas, that "all his house believed in God" with him. So it was one joyous element in the experience of Asked-of-God that she who had joined her life with his had also come to share the new faith and the new hope. An experience of two years as an orthodox missionary in India only helped to confirm her in the importance of practical Christianity over creeds and dogmas. Her sister, who by independent thought and investigation had reached the same conclusion, constituted the third and only other member of the new convert's "house."

Never forgotten will be the bright Sunday morning when the three stood together at the altar of the Unitarian church, and were received into its fellowship. No statement of experience was required, no subscription to a theological creed. The simple constitution of the society was accepted. The welcome of the pastor was earnest and kindly. Not less so was the welcome of the people. It had been said that Unitarians were cold, but there was no evidence of it in the cordial hand-grasp and warm words of the members of the church who gathered around

THE NEW HOME AND THE NEW FAITH. 193

the new-comers at the close of the service. Asked-of-God could not forget the time when he was welcomed to the old Baptist meeting-house. If the joy of the early conversion was more ecstatic or ebullient, that of the second was serene and peaceful, and not less earnest in its purpose.

He did not, however, remain long in the immediate fellowship of the particular church with which he had united. When a boy, he had "played church" on Sunday, and preached extemporized sermons from an extemporized pulpit. He had felt the call to preach, when he joined the Baptist church. Nothing but family responsibilities, which he assumed at the somewhat immature age of nine years, had prevented him from carrying out a cherished plan of preparing himself for the Baptist ministry. The desire to become a minister of religion had never been suppressed. It burst forth into new flame when he joined the Unitarian church. A few months thereafter, he had resigned his position in the State Department, and with satchel in hand and phonographic pencils in his pocket, was speeding on his way to the Cambridge Divinity School.

Of untold value was the opportunity which opened to him here. How he rejoiced in the new friendships he formed, in the inviting and stimulating course of study he pursued, in the companionship and counsel of its learned, generous, and helpful professors, in the rich stores of the library, and all the advantages which life at Cambridge affords, I can indicate, but not describe.

"Ah," said the much-loved orthodox aunt, with a new tone of sorrow, "he has gone to that nest of Unitarians!" But it was a delightful nest in which to hatch a young minister.

The time came when the fledgling must try his wings. Thirteen years before, when yet a mere boy of fifteen, he had stood by the mantelpiece one evening a few months after he had joined the Baptist church. What safer and more sacred place for the dearest and holiest aspirations of a boy's soul than his mother's heart? To this hallowed sacristy he had committed the secret of his purpose to preach the gospel. As he stood in delightful reverie, musing over the possibilities of the future, he said to his mother, "What shall be the text for my first sermon?" There was not a moment's hesitation. Quick as a flash came the response, —

"*God is Love.*"

That text was never written down in any place but the boy's heart. Could it ever be forgotten? It expressed in a single sentence the prime elements in her theology. Loyal Baptist though she was, theological disquisitions and disputes had but little attraction for her. The practical and devotional side of Christianity embodied its doctrinal essence. Her theism was beautifully expressed in this sweet and comprehensive definition of God. When the time came for Asked-of-God to go forth and preach his first sermon, the text written on his heart was easily found in the Bible. Not one letter in it had become dim.

It had survived all the changes in his belief. Many things had passed away, but this still abode in his heart. It was to him a joyful consciousness that the text his mother gave him had only become a stronger and stronger element in the new faith into which he had grown. It was, indeed, the strength of his conviction of the love of God, and its perfect compatibility with eternal justice, which had compelled him to abandon the caricatures of God which disfigured the galleries of the old theology. He could not preach the gospel at all, if he had not full faith in that Eternal Goodness of which Whittier has sung so sweetly in his psalm.

It was a singular coincidence that the church in which he was called upon to preach his first sermon should have been in the birthplace of the prophet of American Unitarianism, William Ellery Channing. Of the sermon delivered on that occasion I have no need to give any report. The text itself was the sermon; and the sermon was the text, "God is Love."

It is ten years since Asked-of-God entered the ministry of the Liberal faith. He has not exhausted its possibilities, neither has he left them untested. And now he may justly be asked to state briefly some aspects of his experience concerning it. As he entered the active duties of the ministry, he was interested to see just what would be the practical working of this new faith, which theologically and ethically seemed so satisfying. Years before, as he sat by the fireside a few nights after his baptism, radiant with the joy of his hope in Christ, an older brother of the church had said to him, " You will enjoy your religion only so long as you live it." That was one test of the old Baptist faith, — a religion that could be lived. There was still another test it offered. It must be a religion which should meet without flinching the terrors of death. So Asked-of-God went forth to his new work with these old questions in his heart: *Is it a religion to live by? Is it a religion to die by?* He had no fear of the response which he should meet. He would not dare test the capacity of the new faith in developing a good life by his own experience. With contrition and shamefacedness, he would be sadly obliged to confess how far short he had fallen of its noble ideals, how he had failed to illustrate them in his own life; but he could confidently answer this question from the lives of others.

Is it a religion to live by? Asked-of-God went out into the world, into the purlieus of trade where selfishness is ever seeking to rise uppermost in the seething whirlpool of competition. He saw strong, earnest men, who laid no claim to devoutness, upholding a high standard of business morality, adding generosity to their love of justice, and exemplifying the spirit of ethical fidelity in all their business relations. He saw men in the height of prosperity bearing themselves in a spirit of love, charity, and humility. He saw others whose wealth seemed to be a golden tide of beneficence which not only turned the wheels of industry, but fed the fountains of education and benevolence, and spread over the land in irrigating fruit-

THE NEW HOME AND THE NEW FAITH. 197

fulness. He saw others who had not wealth giving themselves without reserve to the service of humanity, enlisting in various causes of reform, extending in humble and kindly service the helping hand and speaking the sympathetic word. He saw women as pure as crystal and men as true as steel, living natural, manly and womanly lives.

Yet, again, he wandered into the shady paths of life, and saw those who had met the storms of adversity, and whose worldly fortunes had been wrecked in the critical tempests of life. He saw them bear with uncomplaining fortitude the lightning, the thunder, and the hail. The old tragedy of Job was re-enacted. "The fire of God had fallen from heaven, and burnt the flocks." "A great wind from the wilderness had smote the four corners of the house, and it had fallen." Yet there they stood firm as a rock, unmoved by the calamities which had shattered their fortunes, saying in the spirit, if not in the words, of Job: "The Lord gave, and the Lord taketh away. Blessed be the name of the Lord." He saw them, too, when the wasting hand of sickness had "touched their bone and their flesh," and turned the bountiful joy which comes with good health into unrelenting pain. He saw men and women who did not accept any of the old creeds, who had given up the nightmare of its superstitions, sweetly and beautifully illustrating the faith of a soul which, however racked in body, is at peace with God.

And what did it all mean? It meant that the religion of the new faith was a religion to live by. Whatever it had given up, it was strong in the elements which pertain to the conduct of the life that now is. The calendar can furnish saints no more illustrious than some that were born and reared in the Unitarian faith.

But is it a religion to die by? The writer does not hold that the chief office of religion is to contribute to equanimity of feeling on the dying-bed. The peace which comes in the dying hour ought to be the reward of the good life which has contributed to it. But it was right here that some of his old friends expressed their deepest distrust in his new faith. He pointed them to the noble examples of character it had evolved. They answered, "It may be good to live by; but is it good to die by?" He could not avoid this question. This, too, he answered by no theory, but simply from the well-attested experience of his own ministry. The convincing reply he found at the dying-bed itself. Ah! who shall put into words that deep and spiritual song of trust which has risen like a psalm from the soul in its last hours on earth, and borne those who have heard it, as it were, unto the very threshold of heaven? What minister of the Liberal faith has not gone with his little cup of comfort to the dying-bed, and found a living placid stream of joy flowing from the heart of the dying, so that all he had to offer seemed poor and meagre compared with that which he himself received? Again and again has the preacher marvelled, and said, "I have not found so great faith, no, not in Israel." How can our faith in immortality weaken, when we hold the hand of one who, standing on the very brink of life, catches the rapt vision of the future world and reflects it in the triumphant peace and joy of his own countenance? What courage, what unwavering faith, what glad hope, exhaled from the soul ready to take its flight! In all the records of the heroism with which death has been met, what could exceed in sublimity some of those scenes which Asked-of-God has witnessed in the quiet walks of life or in its terrible and unexpected catastrophes? Young men and maidens, old men and children, in every rank and station, he has seen pass to the great majority, resigning themselves into the hands of God as sweetly as the child falls to sleep in its mother's arms. And when, in the varied experiences which his ministry has brought him, he has seen these beautiful illustrations of faith and hope in the life which now is and in the life which is to come, the peaceful resignation and unclouded affection which forgot no want of others in contemplating its own destiny, the patient heroism of the uncomplaining sufferer through long and weary days and nights of unremitting pain, and finally the glad and triumphant deliverance, he has said in the joy of his own heart, "It is not only a good religion to live by: it is a good religion to die by."

It was on the practical side of the new faith that Asked-of-God discovered its point of union with the old. When he recalled the saintly teacher of the infant school, the sweetness and piety of a beloved mother, the earnest and consecrated lives of many faithful ministers and devoted laymen who professed the faith in which he had been reared, he knew that there was something deeper and more vital in the principle beneath it than that which appeared in the dry husks of its creeds. It was evident, too, that these manifestations of faith, piety, and love were not confined to any one sect or cult. There was no form of Protestantism whose roots did not go down into a soil deeper than that covered by its rites or standards. If Arminianism could point to sweet and noble lives, so could Calvinism. If Protestantism had its gallery of saints, so had Catholicism. If Christianity had its prophets and martyrs, so had Judaism. The same flame of piety which burned on the altar of the Greek illumined the temple of the Hindu. What did it mean but that, deep down beneath all temporal divisions of sect, creed, clime, and age, there is in the very nature of man a sense of a common dependence upon a Higher Power, a recognition of a Supreme Mind and Heart which evokes the sentiment of reverence and piety, and reveals the foundations of an unfailing trust? Beyond all the varied differences in the *forms* of religious faith is the deeper unity furnished by that faith itself. As science affirms one force in nature from which all forms of energy spring, so all forms of religion spring from that one Eternal Life in the soul which makes religion possible.

It was this sense of the universality of the religious principle which prevented Asked-of-God from seeing in the new faith merely a new form of sectarianism. He saw that the old faith and the new had a common ground of reality beneath their varied forms of expression. He

THE NEW HOME AND THE NEW FAITH. 201

rejoiced to see that the piety and practical righteousness of which the old faith was capable, were manifested in the new. But notwithstanding this common ground of reality, the new faith was something more than a mere sequence to the old. It was larger, richer, and, with reference to its adaptation to the life of to-day, a more living faith. The writer cannot close this comparison without indicating briefly a few points in which the new faith seems larger and brighter than the old. The comparison is of course more especially between the faith in which he was reared and that into which he has grown.

1. *The new faith is one allied to freedom.* Limitation, not freedom, is the characteristic of the old theology. The Church has feared the possible results of unlimited liberty of thought. It has raised barriers, forged manacles, issued prohibitions, and circumscribed the bounds of free inquiry. It has assumed that faith and freedom cannot exist together. It has distrusted science, and been suspicious of philosophy. It has resorted to infallible books, popes, and councils as the source of its authority. The new faith assumes that faith and freedom are not antagonistic, but mutually helpful. It assures perfect liberty of investigation in every department of human thought. It gives free rein to science and philosophy. It has no fear that they can undermine or supplant religion, for its foundations rest upon eternal reality. The only barriers to human thought and investigation are those which are furnished by the natural limitations and the finite powers of

the human mind. "Where the Spirit of God is, there is liberty." Thus the new faith is one which thrives in the open air. Freedom of growth is necessary to its healthy existence.

2. *The new faith is adjusted to a larger light than the old.* Pastor Robinson's words have been fulfilled. More light has broken forth from the Divine word. Leaders in every department of science and thought have smitten the rocks by the way. New fountains of knowledge have burst forth to refresh the mind and heart of man. Nothing has been more marvellous during the last century than the growth of the scientific spirit, and the large and fruitful results it has achieved. There is scarcely any department of study which has not been wonderfully enriched by exact and laborious research. The supposed foundations of knowledge, on which many of the deductions of the old faith were based, have been disturbed and displaced. Much that was supposed to be real, under the searching light of fearless inquiry, has been proved to be mythical and legendary. But in many cases where science has removed the shifting sand, it has shown us a deeper bed-rock of reality beneath. If it reveals here and there the weakness of the flimsy and decaying bridges which the old faith had courageously thrown over fathomless problems, the new faith is able to build safer and broader and freer highways.

As the monkish guardians of the old faith feared the results of freedom, so they feared the diffusion of too much light. Their religious beliefs and the authority they derived from them seemed to thrive better in the darkness of superstition than under the light of knowledge. Many of the standards of Protestantism are similarly mediæval; they cannot be harmonized with our present knowledge of the constitution of the physical world, or the constitution of humanity. The current theology is based upon supposed statements of fact and history in Semitic books, and upon primitive notions of ethics and society which have long since been outgrown. The old theology has not been adjusted to the light of to-day. To be persuaded of its correctness, one must see it in the dimmer light and with the imperfect lenses of a bygone age. It is the characteristic of the new theology, that it adjusts itself to every new sunrise of divine revelation. The fruit of the tree of knowledge is one calculated to make men wise. It is a tree which cannot grow in the darkness. It is one of the precious trees in the garden, and no flaming cherubim forbid the approach of the hungry mind. Whatever light shines upon the page of history or illumines the landscape of the external world, revealing more truly the conditions of our physical existence; whatever light shines upon the mind of man, stimulating its growth and guiding its operations; whatever light floods the human heart with its awakening influence, unfolding new sources of affection, and indicating new pathways of duty, — is welcomed by the new faith as a part of the ever-unfolding revelation of Divine truth.

The cautious timidity of advocates of the old theology about accepting the positive and indubitable results of modern science and modern criticism is the confession of weakness in the very groundwork of their faith. The Mosaic cosmology, the legend of Joshua stopping the sun, the literal story of the Garden of Eden, the imperfect tribal notions of the Hebrews concerning God, and even the Bible chronology itself have all been stoutly defended against more rational and more truthful interpretations which the light of to-day renders possible and necessary. The writer knows full well that there were many in the old meeting-house who would have felt that a serious blow had been dealt at the foundations of religion, if the literal statement of Genesis that the world was made in six days were at all questioned. Such irrational defenders of the old faith are becoming less and less common. Relief has been partly found by more ingenious interpretations; but full and perfect relief is only secured when it is seen that infallibility can no longer be predicated of religious records, and that under the light of reason the facts which science reveals are not dissonant with the truths of religion. The mediæval attitude of the Church towards new light was not only inhospitality, but positive enmity. It feared that its canons of authority would be displaced. It lighted the fires of persecution, and condemned to the rack and the prison those who proclaimed the truths they had discovered. It mattered not whether it was a truth relating to physical science or one which related immediately to theology. Galileo's assertion that the earth moved was as heretical as Luther's assertion of justification by faith. With the advent and development of Protestantism, the right of private judgment and a rational principle were applied to religious discussions. But Protestantism had not sufficient courage to trust its own principles. It feared the effect of too much light. It rightly wished to preserve all that was substantial and nourishing in the old faith; but in doing so, it accepted and insisted upon elements which were not necessary to its vitality. It did not distinguish between the permanent and transient elements in religion. Hence many of the statements and creeds of modern Protestantism are like the sensitive paper of the photographer; they turn black when exposed to the sunlight of to-day.

It is one of the distinguishing attributes of the new faith, therefore, that it is reasonable. It does not disown facts, on the one side, or logic on the other. There were few things more gratifying to the writer than the assured consciousness which came to him that religious faith could be at once rational and spiritual. An obstinate insistence upon the irrational claims of the old theology has alienated many from the pathways of religion. It is the work of the new faith to reclaim them; and this it does by assuring them that religion is not opposed to reason or knowledge, — that it welcomes liberty, and comes to new bloom and fruitage in the light.

3. *The new faith has a larger and loftier ethical basis.* Ethics, like science, is capable of progress in its interpretation and application. The old theology had indeed an ethical basis. It made much of righteousness in God and righteousness in man, but its notions of righteousness were

confused and contradictory. The righteousness of God was of a different kind from the righteousness of man. The righteousness necessary for admission to heaven was different from that which was necessary for moral excellence on earth. It is not only the irrational elements, but also the defective ethical elements, in most of the old creeds and standards which alienate many who once held them. Arminianism was largely a protest against the false ethics of Calvinism. It is not necessary here to point out in detail the ethical difficulties connected with accepting the Calvinistic notion of God. Dr. Channing has done it in his powerful essay on the moral argument against Calvinism. Calvinism was a conception of God as absolute power; the new faith conceives him to be absolute righteousness. In the standards of the old system we can see the evidences of a rude, primitive, and even barbaric notion of the Deity. Practical views of morality in the relations of men with one another have made greater progress in the old theology than ethical conceptions concerning God. The moral difficulties of the old system have been freely admitted by its advocates. Many desperate attempts have been made to reconcile them with enlightened views of divine justice; but their most consistent defenders have been compelled to fall back upon the assumed authority of an infallible revelation. Thus, in regard to the subject of everlasting punishment, the question which many Calvinists ask is not, Is it rational or is it just, but simply is it taught in the Bible?

From nothing has the new faith received a greater impulse than from more enlightened and progressive ethical conceptions. Channing spoke none too strongly when he said of the Calvinistic view of God that "it darkens and stains his pure nature, spoils his character of its sacredness, loveliness, glory, and thus quenches the central light of the universe, makes existence a curse, and the extinction of it a consummation devoutly to be wished." The enlightened faith of to-day, while it preserves all that was strongest and best in the Calvinistic view of God, is no longer troubled by the dark shadows which the old view casts upon the Divine perfections. The new faith embodies a higher idea of Divine righteousness. It is no less strenuous in its application of ethics to human life. It concedes that the highest object of a human life is to develop perfection of character in itself and others. All that human experience and the inspiration of the noblest leaders of the race have revealed in regard to the law of justice, it accepts as active moral authority. But as it looks forward for fresh acquisitions of knowledge and the development of a keener and more far-reaching intelligence, so it expects still further illuminations of moral truth which shall reveal more clearly the pathway of duty and point more certainly to the goal of a perfect life.

4. *The new faith is founded upon a more perfect conception of Divine love.* Love is one of the key-notes of the old faith. It was the love of God that sent Jesus into the world, that provided for the redemption of humanity, that chose a certain number to be saved from the everlasting

penalties of sin. When we look back to the primitive Christian Church and read the beautiful Epistle of John, we see how mighty was the influence of love in that Christian brotherhood, and how exalted a place it held in the conception of God. But the mediæval theology discrowned it. The love of God which shines through Calvinism was not the love of God for humanity, but simply his love for a small portion of the human race which he had chosen to be saved. It almost obliterated that conception of the Divine fatherhood which Jesus so beautifully held, and which shines out with genial warmth in other religions. The new faith restores and re-crowns this grand and holy conception of the Divine love. It no longer limits it. Once more it shines upon the evil and the good. God is no longer seen to be the special guardian of any chosen portion of the race. He is the Universal Father of humanity, and his goodness shines beneficently through his universal laws.

Those who, like the writer, have been reared in the old theology, especially that of the Calvinistic school, will admit the terrible strain it made upon the affections. Few things are more pathetic than the mournful cries which went up from many who held the old creeds when they vividly pictured the eternal destiny of those who were near and dear to them. Heaven could not be enjoyed so long as such a conviction persisted. Jonathan Edwards could only hold out the hope that this natural affection would perish. The mother who laid her little babe away in the graveyard was sometimes reproached by the feeling,

THE NEW HOME AND THE NEW FAITH. 209

which conscientious ministers did not hesitate to encourage, that she had loved her little one too much, and that a jealous God had taken away her idol. The more perfect love of the new faith casts out fear. It assures the mother that it is not possible to love her offspring too much; that her love for it is but another manifestation of gratitude to Him who has called it into being.

The love for humanity inspired by the old faith has sent earnest and self-sacrificing missionaries across the seas to carry the gospel to the heathen. The new faith looks with tenderness and sympathy upon all efforts for the amelioration of humanity; but instead of picturing the heathen as pouring in vast and innumerable cataracts into everlasting misery, it sees them as the children of a universal Father, sharing the privileges, the hopes, and the destiny of our common humanity. To put by cruel, unjust, and barbaric notions of God in his relations to humanity, and to substitute larger and more cheerful and inspiring views of the Divine government, is to open again the fountains of charity in the human heart, to give a new impulse to the spirit of beneficence, and to renew the bonds of universal brotherhood. In the highest conceptions of God, love and justice are reconciled. And it is the work of the advocates of the new faith to illustrate and to reconcile these principles in human society.

Liberty, Light, Righteousness, Love, — these are the essential and inspiring elements of the new faith. If it be said that they are also implied in the old, we shall not contest the claim, for the new is but a fuller and more natural development of the old. The old faith was the faith of yesterday; the new is the faith of to-day. And when we compare it with that which it has outgrown, we see that its liberty is larger, its light more abundant, its righteousness more perfect, and its love more universal.

XXV.

CONCLUSION.

IT is but a twelvemonth since Asked-of-God found himself one Sunday morning in his native city of New York. I do not know what influence it was which touched the chord of the old association; but some interest stronger, I am sure, than mere curiosity led him to seek the church which had been his first spiritual home. The society had long since left the old Baptist meeting-house; and the building, as I have previously said, had been turned into a public school. As a society, it had resisted the tide of movement which carried its principal rival, the Norfolk Street Church, up to Fifth Avenue. It had even gone farther south; and its church building was in the seventh ward, among the homes of the poor. It was just at the hour of half-past ten that Asked-of-God entered the house. He had often passed the building as a child on his way to the infant class in the Olive Branch Church. At that time it was used as a Congregational church, and the little boy had only a feeble idea what that meant. As he now for the first time entered the building on this Sunday morning, the interior was strange to him, but not stranger than the faces that he saw. He missed the familiar form and ringing voice of his pastor in the pulpit. Where was old Brother C., with his oscillating head nodding his verdict on the sermon from his judgment box in the pew? Where were Deacon B. and Deacon W. and a score of others? Where the faithful band of sisters who were never absent from their pews? The house was scarcely half full. How different from the old revival days, in the old building, when every pew from floor to gallery was crowded, and chairs had to be brought into the aisles!

As the visitor stood in the doorway trying vainly to pick up some thread of association which should lead him back to old and familiar emotions, a man of about his own age came forward, and offered him a seat. No sooner did the visitor's eye fall upon him than it kindled with recognition. Yes; here was one of his old Sunday-school mates. They had sat in the same class together; they had joined the church during the same revival. Notwithstanding all the changes through which Asked-of-God had passed, there was a precious memory in this old bond.

"Don't you know me?" he asked.

The usher paused, took a searching look, and said with a smile and the old-time fervor, "Yes, it is Asked-of-God." (It was a long time since the visitor had been called by his Hebrew name.)

"But where are the old members?"

The history of the more prominent ones was briefly told. Some had moved up town, protesting against the action of the church in refusing to go as a society; some had gone to Brooklyn, Jersey, and to West Chester; some had fallen from grace; and many had been laid away to rest.

"I am about the only one of the old band left," said the usher.

So far as Asked-of-God was concerned, the old Baptist meeting-house and all the associations which made it precious had passed away from him as truly as he had passed away from it. Nothing could restore it. The building had been put to other uses, and those who once worshipped in it had been scattered far and near. The society was like a knife with a new blade and a new handle. Nothing but the name remained.

As Asked-of-God left the old church, it was in a meditative but not in a melancholy mood. He felt perhaps somewhat as Paul felt when he wrote the third chapter of second Corinthians. Paul recognized the fact that some things had passed away, and that they had passed away so completely that they could not be restored. They were things that he had once loved. He had been raised a Jew. He had been educated at the feet of Gamaliel; he knew the Jewish law in all its detail of precept and ceremonial. Around that history and the institutions which it represented, there was a certain halo of glory, which to him was by no means fictitious. Then, as he wrote that chapter, he looked back upon these institutions which he had once loved. He saw the marks of fulfilment and decay written upon them. If Paul had looked only at this fact, it would have been a very melancholy reflection for him. But it was not Saul the Jew who was speaking: it was Paul the Christian. And for Paul the Christian, this thought was saddened by no touch of regret; for he saw that as the sun of Judaism had set, the sun of Christianity had arisen, and the glory of that which had come eclipsed the glory of that which had passed away.

So it was with Asked-of-God. Much had passed away, much also remained; and the glory of that which remained was greater than that which had passed away.

As he parted with his friend and left the church on this Sunday morning, he felt indeed that the old temple had gone. But a new temple had arisen in its stead. His face was toward the rising sun. He saw in his mind's eye

The New Baptist Meeting-House.

It seemed so beautiful and so grand to eye and heart that he forgot the glory of the old in rejoicing in the glory of the new. I know that I cannot do justice to it in any description that I may give. We cannot wholly describe all there is of to-day in the realities about us, but the new Baptist meeting-house belongs also to the morrow. Its foundations are deeply laid in reality, but its superstructure rises like a prophecy into the domain of the ideal and the unattained.

It is not something that can be wholly described by measurement. The rod of Ezekiel cannot determine its proportions. Its architecture is attractive and pleasant, but not wholly from its external quality. It embodies a soul. "The conscious stone to beauty grew." It is not dominated wholly by one style; for it is spirit, not form, that makes the temple. It may be Gothic, Romanesque, or modern in its outline and detail, but it is not grotesque. Its very architecture is marked by catholicity. It rejects nothing true or beautiful because it is old, nothing true or beautiful because it is new. The building itself is an architectural psalm. No one who sees the new Baptist meeting-house mistakes it for a circus or a skating-rink. The outward form suggests the inward spirit. It seems to the beholder to be a house of God, and yet it is unmistakably also a house for man. It is not closed during the week. There is no time in the busy working hours of the day when the worshipper may not enter its courts for silent meditation, communion, or praise. No foreign or frivolous trespass is allowed to break the spell of that association which comes from the consecration of one place to the holiest emotions. Yet in other parts of the building there is ample provision for all useful and helpful forms of social and benevolent activity. There are reading and class rooms for the studious; for education is one part of the work of the new Baptist meeting-house. There are other rooms devoted to charitable work. There is a spacious chapel with class-rooms for the Sunday-school, and ample parlors for social gatherings. The church during the week is not like a deserted barn. It is radiant with activity.

Its terms of membership are not described by any tests of doctrinal belief. It welcomes all to its fellowship who sympathize with its spirit and who would share its activities. Not uniformity of belief, but perfection of character, is the end which it has set before itself. It seeks to solve for men the practical problem of life, and to reconcile them to the Truth, the Beauty, and the Goodness which blend like prismatic colors in the being of God.

If it is not always defining its belief and tinkering its creed, there are nevertheless great positive and vital truths which command its convictions and inspire its activity. One of these grand truths is the marvellous power which is wrapped up in the name of God. In the new Baptist meeting-house it matters not so much how that name is spelled. It is the ever-present and abiding reality it expresses, the "infinite and eternal energy" of thought and love, which charge it with significance. God is not simply a creator, not an artisan. He is the Eternal Life, the soul of the universe. The human heart still calls him Father and Mother. These are but images through which the soul expresses its kinship with the Eternal. The will of God is simply the Eternal Righteousness fulfilling itself. Human love must find its origin in the Divine heart from which it is born. Human life is no longer to be moulded to the theological scheme of the old pattern. God is not cruel nor vindictive, nor agitated by human passions. He is not jealous, capricious, or revengeful. He is not an unrelenting Shylock or an unmerciful Nero. He is Truth, Beauty, and Love. He is the life "in whom we live and move and have our being." He is not far from every one of us, for we are all his offspring.

With the truth of God there is the truth of sonship. Humanity is not lost, fallen, degraded, or disowned. It is the life of God coming into consciousness, freedom, development in the life of man. Sin is not the result of the appetite of a fabled progenitor in a primitive garden: it is the imperfection of the child that has not grown to full stature; it is the force of animal, selfish, and uncorrected instincts, which have come up from the savage life, which time and growth, the law of reward and the law of penalty and the force of spiritual renovation, can alone subdue.

As the new Baptist meeting-house has its God ideal, so it has its Christ ideal. Its Christ is not a matter of tradition, textual criticism, punctuation marks. It is the manifestation of God in the flesh. It is the sublime truth of the incarnation not localized, but made universal. Not only Jesus, but all the spiritually good and beautiful, all who have enriched humanity by golden precept or divine example, are transfigured into one likeness in this Christ ideal. As the photographer can take the likeness of a score or more of persons superimposed upon the plate until he has secured the typical likeness of the whole group, so the Christ ideal is the typical likeness of the perfect man.

The worshippers in the new Baptist meeting-house find inspiration in the great law of sacrifice. As they lift the eye of gratitude toward God for his blessings, so they turn with gratitude toward humanity. They recognize and bless the martyrs and heroes of the race. They honor and reverence the names of all who have illustrated the law of love in their lives, witnessed with unfaltering fidelity the truth that was revealed to them, and taught humanity that only by divine self-forgetfulness can it rise to its highest life. And if, among all the sons of men who have lived and died for humanity, Jesus of Nazareth commands the highest homage, it is because humanity has said that he is worthy of it. There is no longer any dispute about his rank, no longer a quarrel as to how much of God and how much of humanity his nature contains. He is the son of a human father and a human mother. By the lineage of the flesh, by all the passions and temptations, the sufferings and victories that pertain to human life, he is our elder brother; and yet he unfolds so richly and marvellously the spiritual possibilities of our nature that we call him without estrangement or contradiction the Son of Man and the Son of God, — "for as many as are led by the spirit of God they are the sons of God."

As the new Baptist meeting-house has a firm foundation in the realities of the present, so its faith and its hope unfold the vision of immortal life. The fear of death casts no shadows over its altars. That the body of clay may turn to dust, that all that is tangible and material in the physical world may eventually perish, is a matter of no concern. The soul that is born of God shall return unto the life that gave it. The Eternal Life itself is the pledge of our immortality. This consciousness of an immortal life does not interfere with the present duties of its members. It gives to that word "duty" something more than a local and temporal meaning: it links it to that which is enduring. There is strength and comfort, admonition and inspiration, in the thought that the present life is the prelude to a life to come, — a new opportunity for rectification, growth, fulfilment. The heaven which is looked for in the new Baptist meeting-house is not altogether the heaven of the old one, not a white-robed orchestra, not a heaven of unceasing monotony. It is the same tireless search for truth, the hunger after righteousness, the joy of reconciliation with God. It is the endless progress of the soul toward perfection and its ceaseless ministry of love.

And what shall I say of the worship, forms, ceremonies, and rituals of this renewed Baptist meeting-house? Simply that they are varied and flexible enough to suit the needs of those who adopt them. If its walls are decorated by the hand of art, it is not merely to please the eye, but to inspire the soul. If music rises from choir and transept, it is that devotion may be expressed and also awakened. If a liturgy is used, it is not because some church council prescribed it, but because it fits the spirit and fervor of worship. In the form of its worship as in the form of its art, and in the spirit of its religion, the church is catholic. It gathers prayers and precepts, living words and burning thoughts, from the saints and seers of all time. It stops not to think of age or clime. The pillar of fire has moved along through the centuries before the people of God, and cast its revealing light over many lands. What matters it whose rod has smitten the rock, so long as the living waters flow?

The Bible of the new Baptist meeting-house is the slowly written Bible of the ages. Greek and Hindu, Christian and Jew, people of all kindreds and climes, utter its language. The Hebrew and the Christian Bibles have not been dethroned. They are no longer a fetich or a talisman, but an inspiration. They are a priceless part of the sacred literature of the world. The facts they record are tried by the tests of science, history, and criticism; but their spiritual and moral truths are verified by the experience of the human heart. In the new Baptist meeting-house the Bible is read with the reason, judgment, and sympathy which should be applied to all books. The written Word is but a part of the larger discourse of God which is ever revealing itself to the heart of man.

There is "close communion" in the new Baptist meeting-house; but it is the closeness of sympathy, not the closeness of exclusion. There is baptism there, but it is rather the baptism of fire than the baptism of water. The law of its discipline is the law of charity; the law of its life, the perfect law of liberty, duty, and love.

Such was the vision of the new Baptist meeting-house that came to Asked-of-God. I have not given all that came to his eye, nor could I give it with the warmth of emotion with which it came to his heart. Another eye would see many things perhaps that he has not seen; for the new Baptist meeting-house looks a little different from each point of the compass. It is not a village meeting-house; it is not the church of a sect: it is the temple of the Church Universal. It shelters many different heads and hearts. The light that glows in its "storied windows richly dight" reveals many different pictures, — some the record of its saints and martyrs, others the visions of its prophets. Its walls are built of many stones, but they are cemented together by an indissoluble faith. Variety and diversity express its comprehensiveness; but the deeper truth it utters is that of *unity*, — one God, one faith, one baptism, — the unity of the spirit in the bond of peace. This is the *Unit*-arianism of the new Baptist meeting-house.

Ezekiel, when he experienced his wondrous vision of the temple, was taken up by the Spirit, and brought into the inner court; and, "behold, the glory of the Lord filled the house." So the uplifting vision came to Asked-of-God; and when he had compared the new temple with the old one, whose veil had been rent in twain, he felt like saying, in the words of Paul, —

"*If that which is done away was glorious, much more that which remaineth is glorious.*"

www.ingramcontent.com/pod-product-compliance
Lightning Source LLC
Chambersburg PA
CBHW021846230426
43669CB00008B/1094